The Scalable Business Framework™

THE SCALABLE BUSINESS FRAMEWORK™
How to Build a Business You Love While Enjoying Your Life (A Business Fable)

Copyright © 2025 John Burdett and Michael A. Johnson

ISBN: 978-1-964046-70-9

This publication is designed to provide accurate and authoritative information regarding the subject matter contained within. It should be understood that the author and publisher are not engaged in rendering legal, accounting, or other financial services through this medium. The author and publisher shall not be liable for your misuse of this material and shall have neither liability nor responsibility to anyone with respect to any loss or damage caused, or alleged to be caused, directly or indirectly by the information contained in this book. The author and/or publisher do not guarantee that anyone following these strategies, suggestions, tips, ideas, or techniques will become successful. If legal advice or other expert assistance is required, the services of a competent professional should be sought.

All rights reserved. No portion of this book may be reproduced mechanically, electronically, or by any other means, including photocopying, without the written permission of the author. It is illegal to copy the book, post it to a website, or distribute it by any other means without permission from the author.

Expert Press
11610 Pleasant Ridge Rd.
Suite 103, #189
Little Rock, AR 72223
www.ExpertPress.net

Editing by Elaina Robbins
Copyediting by Hannah Skaggs
Proofreading by Geena Barret
Text design and composition by Emily Fritz
Cover design by Casey Fritz

The Scalable Business Framework™

How to Build a Business You Love While Enjoying Your Life

(A Business Fable)
John Burdett and Michael A. Johnson

*To our families, teammates,
and great clients at Fast Slow Motion.*

Contents

Introduction by John Burdett ... 1

Part 1: The Tipping Point — 5
1. A Successful Mess ... 7
2. The Mentor ... 21

Part 2: The Three P's — 27
3. Purpose ... 29
4. Leadership ... 53
5. Team ... 83
6. Clients, Mentorships, and Business Partners ... 111
7. Profit ... 137

Part 3: The Scalable Business Framework — 169
8. Strategic Objectives ... 171
9. Systems and Processes ... 193
10. Processes and CRMs ... 221
11. Automation ... 247
12. Visibility ... 273

Part 4: Impact — 295
13. A New Dawn ... 297

Conclusion by Michael A. Johnson ... 305
Afterword by John Burdett ... 307
Recommended Reading ... 317
About the Authors ... 321

Introduction

By John Burdett

Back when I was in my twenties, about four or five years into my career, I made a terrible mistake that haunts me to this day. I helped scale a company and had around one hundred people reporting to me, and my wife Misty and I had already started having kids.

When my daughter was born in May 2004, I did what most dads do: I stayed at the hospital and slept in the little chair next to my wife for a few days. The birth went smoothly, and everyone was delighted to meet Kenna. Then, as my wife was recovering, I got a phone call from an important client asking for a meeting.

Misty and Kenna seemed fine. This was an important client, and I wanted the business. So, I agreed to schedule the meeting for 3:00 p.m. the next day.

As soon as I got off the phone, the doctor walked into the room.

"Congratulations," she said. "You can take Kenna home tomorrow at 3:00 p.m."

And guess what? I kept the meeting.

I cringe looking back on that moment. I prioritized work over my family, and I'll always regret that I wasn't there to take my daughter home from the hospital. Looking back now, I have no idea what the meeting was about, who it was with, or whether it was even productive. That's how "important" it actually turned out to be. Decisions like these have long-term consequences, and you can't undo them. Luckily, I have a very forgiving and loving wife, but to this day, I'm still haunted by my selfishness and the pain I caused her.

These are the types of unnecessary and injurious sacrifices we make as business leaders without considering the long-term consequences. In that moment, even sitting in the hospital with my postpartum wife and newborn daughter, I was focused on the wrong thing. I was so caught up in the need to excel—to take care of everything and everyone—that I lost sight of what truly mattered.

Thankfully, with some thoughtful changes and the help of wise mentors along the way, I was able to find success in business without sacrificing the important things. And I want to help others do the same. This is one of the reasons I do what I do today.

My company, Fast Slow Motion, helps entrepreneurs scale their businesses without missing out on all of the other important things in life. Since 2014, we've helped thousands of clients transform their businesses and their lives by implementing systems and processes that empower them to scale up while allowing the leaders to focus *on* the business instead of being trapped *in* the business. Now, with *The Scalable Business Framework*, we can help an even wider audience.

If you're like a lot of business owners I know, you don't just want to be excellent at business—you want to be a great parent, spouse, sibling, friend—all of it. Fast Slow Motion's director of growth, Michael Johnson, and I wrote this book for business owners and leaders who strive to scale and grow their businesses while excelling in other areas of their lives. This book is my life's story and my life's work all rolled into one. It provides a framework for improving your business and achieving balance in a business fable format, featuring a protagonist who exemplifies all these common issues and a mentor who helps him turn everything around. In this story, I'm both Tim and Barry—just at different times in my life.

Maybe your business is a few months old, or maybe you've been doing this for years. Either way, your ambition, excellence, and hard work have gotten you to where you are today. You're likely successful on the outside, but you may feel trapped in your business and unbalanced in different areas of your life. *The Scalable Business Framework* will show you how to break free from the chaos, start enjoying life again, and really have it all. I've done it, my clients have done it, and now it's your turn.

Part 1

The Tipping Point

Chapter 1

A Successful Mess

"Mr. Hodges, we're so pleased to include you in this year's Birmingham 40 Under 40 list. Congratulations once again on this outstanding achievement."

The reporter, smiling, settles back in one of the chairs in front of Tim's large executive desk. The corner office on the nineteenth floor offers a lovely view of downtown Birmingham, where many Christmas displays are glittering in the afternoon sun. Tim thinks it will all look splendid on camera, and with both a videographer and a photographer present, the *Birmingham Live* crew is bound to catch some good shots.

He adjusts the lapel microphone on his tailored gray suit and straightens his navy tie, smiling broadly.

"Thank you, Ralph," he says. "Please, call me Tim."

"All right, if you insist," Ralph says, pulling out a few papers and spreading them on the edge of the desk. "Now, let's get started. Remember to look at me and not at the camera, okay?"

The reporter pauses, his smile growing even broader as he focuses on the camera.

"Hello, folks. Today, we're here with Tim Hodges, the owner of FastTrack Home Services. Although he's only thirty-three years old, Mr. Hodges has taken his company from a team of seven or so to a team of thirty, with plans to double that in the next two years. Is that correct, Tim?"

"Yes, that's right, Ralph," Tim says, his grin freezing as his computer pings with an incoming email. He quickly hits the mute button, watching out of the corner of his eye as emails start to pile up faster than he can count.

Ugh, he thinks. *Now what?*

"Brilliant," Ralph says. "Tell us a little about FastTrack Home Services, Tim."

"We're a full-service HVAC provider working with homeowners," Tim says. "In the next few years, we're hoping to expand to commercial applications and start offering plumbing and electrical."

But that takes organization and planning, he thinks. *And since I'm always in disaster mode, who knows when or even if that can happen?*

"Unlike a lot of other HVAC businesses," he continues out loud, "we employ our own HVAC technicians full-time along with administrative support staff, ensuring quality service every time."

As he talks, Tim spots something red on the floor. Glancing down, he sees with horror that a protein bar wrapper is lying on the rug next to his foot. As nonchalantly as he can, he uses his foot to scoot the offending wrapper behind his wastepaper bin and out of sight of the cameras, wincing as it makes a slight crackling noise.

"That's wonderful," Ralph says, a subtle downward dart of his gaze confirming to Tim that his covert move has absolutely been noticed. "Now, I understand that you aren't the founder of this business. Tell us how you ended up in the CEO's office."

Tim automatically gestures to the triptych-style photo frame on the wall next to the desk, and the camera pivots to focus.

"See that last photo?" Tim asks, indicating the picture of himself looking young and energetic, with his arms around Bertha, a tiny, wrinkled woman in a business suit. Both of them are laughing uproariously.

Thank God you can't see me now, Bertha, Tim thinks.

"Wow, you look so young there!" Ralph exclaims. "What are you, seventeen?"

"Close," Tim says. "That's me at twenty." He looks enviously at the smooth face and flat torso in the photo. He played high school baseball and continued in Birmingham University's recreational baseball league, but now he can't remember the last time he hit the gym. The buttons of his dress shirt seem to strain against his belly with every breath.

"Who's that lovely lady you're with?" asks Ralph leadingly.

"That's Bertha Manning, the founder of FastTrack Home Services," Tim says proudly, snapping back to attention. "Bertha was a close family friend. When I was growing up, she was always around—very active in my church too. She had no children of her own, and when I told her I was studying business at Birmingham U, she immediately asked me to do a summer internship with her. I did that every summer and never looked back."

"Very heartwarming," Ralph says. "Is she a role model of yours?"

"Yes," Tim says. "She was a great lady. She really took me under her wing and taught me everything I know about building custom HVAC solutions for homes, both new builds and renovation projects."

"When did you take over for Ms. Manning?"

"When her health started to fail at age seventy-seven or so, she finally retired," Tim says. "She wished she could stay forever, I swear! Leaving the business was really hard for her, but it was time. I was twenty-five then, and she passed away three years later, after a stroke."

Tim looks at the picture again, at Bertha's laughing face and crinkled eyes. He wants to make her proud. Instead, things always seem to be spiraling out of control.

"Now tell me about those other two photos," Ralph says, gesturing at the wall again. "That must be your beautiful family."

Tim looks at the other photos, forcing the smile to remain on his face. There's a picture of him and Robin on their wedding day, both twenty-two and practically glowing with happiness.

"Yes, that's my wife Robin. We met at Birmingham U," Tim says. He holds in a sigh as he looks at Robin's glowing face. When was the last time she looked that happy?

"And those must be your children," Ralph says pointedly after the long, awkward pause.

"Yes, sorry," Tim says, looking at the third photo. "Those are my kids, Genna, Pete, and Christa. They were around six, three, and maybe six months old there, but that was three years ago." In the photo, Genna is smiling hard in her little blue dress, staring determinedly at the camera while Pete pokes her in the ear, his tiny tie askew. Christa is laughing, watching her siblings.

That was supposed to be a family session, Tim thinks bleakly. He had to cancel to make a client meeting instead, and the fight he had with Robin that evening was particularly nasty.

"What a stunning family," Ralph says. "I know this is looking far ahead, but do you think any of your kids will inherit your entrepreneurial spirit?"

Tim doesn't answer immediately. He's distracted by his marketing head, Gina, who has just begun to pace in front of the glass doors to the office.

"Mr. Hodges?" Ralph says, sounding a little annoyed now.

"Oh, yes, sorry," Tim says. His screen is going absolutely ballistic with emails, and he hurriedly turns it off. "What did you say?"

A disgruntled Ralph asks, "Do you think any of your children will take over the business someday?"

"Oh God, I hope not," Tim mutters without thinking.

"Sorry?" Ralph asks.

"Oh, I hope so!" Tim says with artificial brightness. "You're right, it's a little early to tell, but my kids are taking after me already. Both of my older kids play baseball, which is really fun for me. I played in high school."

"How wonderful," Ralph says. "I bet you can offer them lots of coaching in that case."

"All the time," Tim says, a guilty weight settling in his gut. When was the last time he'd been able to even attend a game? He takes a moment to scowl at Gina, only to see that she's been joined by two more members of his staff, who are now huddled outside his office, looking anxious.

What the heck is going on? Can't these people survive twenty minutes without me?

By the time the interview is over, it seems like half of Tim's staff is gathered. They stand clustered together, smiling and waving feebly as the disgruntled-looking news staff file out, passing the all-white Christmas display.

"Thanks again," the receptionist says cheerily, opening the door for them. "Have a wonderful afternoon."

There was dead silence as the door creaked shut. Then all hell broke loose.

"Mr. Hodges, this is a PR nightmare—"

"—need to clear this with you immediately, I remember last time you said—"

"—the numbers just aren't adding up here, and the CPA told me—"

"Shut up!" Tim bellows. Silence reigns.

"Gina, you were first. Come on."

As he shuffles back into his office, Tim looks in the mirror on the wall and instantly regrets it. He has dark bags under his eyes and premature wrinkles that give his face a haggard, drooping appearance. His skin looks paunchy and pale.

Gross, he laments silently as he sits back down at his desk with a sigh, automatically opening a drawer and pulling out a protein bar.

"Mr. Hodges," Gina says, striding in and closing the door. She stops abruptly when she sees his face. "Are you feeling okay? You don't look so good."

"Nice to hear that after I've just been on TV and in a bunch of photos," Tim snaps, glaring at her.

She presses her mouth together in a thin line. "Sorry."

"What do you want?"

"I have bad news."

"What other kind of news is there?" Tim grumbles, staring bleary-eyed at his overflowing inbox and feeling a splitting headache starting to form behind his eyes.

"That one client left us a Google review. You know, the one whose rooftop unit fell through the ceiling four days after installation."

Tim groans and leans over his desk, letting his forehead rest on it.

"How bad is it?"

"Bad. The review is trending."

Tim says nothing. He finds himself wondering vaguely whether he could just sink through the desk and disappear into the floor. His company seems to be spiraling out of control. His employees hate him. Even his wife and kids seem to hate him. And now, apparently, his customers hate him too. To be honest, he kind of agrees with all of them.

"We could try appealing to Google to get it taken down," Gina says after a long silence.

"Did they say anything that wasn't true?" Tim asks the desktop miserably.

"Well, no."

"Then don't bother. Let's just issue a public apology. They already got a refund."

"Okay, then," Gina says. Without moving his head, Tim waves a hand in dismissal. He knows this is rude, but he honestly doesn't have the energy to do anything else.

"Next," he says wearily, as each employee that enters brings another problem for him to solve.

* * *

It's eight thirty by the time Tim pulls up to his house, which twinkles merrily with golden Christmas lights. He's completely and utterly exhausted. He has just spent the past five hours (or, honestly, five years) putting out business fire after business fire. He feels like there's no consistency or predictability to his business operations, as all he can ever do is put out these constant fires. Plus, he feels completely out of control because he never has time to sit down and think about long-term planning or crunch the numbers to make sure he's on track.

He sees instantly that Robin's car isn't there, and his heart sinks. *Oh, no. Was I supposed to go to something this evening?* He scrambles to look at his phone. Eleven missed calls and thirty-five text messages.

Just as he starts to scroll through the disaster, Robin's Lexus pulls in smoothly next to his BMW, the glare of the lights hitting him accusingly. Stuffing his phone back into his pocket, Tim takes a deep breath and opens the door as his family piles out of the Lexus.

"Daddy, where were you?" Genna asks. She's wearing a fluffy white dress and holding a halo headband. Pete, also dressed in all white and clutching a sheep mask, stands next to her in solidarity. Christa, looking ridiculously cute in a tiny red-and-green elf costume, runs around from the other side of the car, takes one look at Tim, and starts yelling in a high, screechy voice.

"Bad daddy! Bad daddy! Bad daddy!"

Robin rounds the SUV, looking beautiful in a forest-green dress and red scarf. The scowl she gives Tim is enough to make him want to get back in his car and drive away.

"Where was I, honey?" Tim says, looking at his daughter. "I was at work. One of my employees is out sick, and I'm having to do a lot more than usual. You all look very nice, by the way."

Genna crosses her arms. "You promised," she says quietly. "You promised you'd come to the Christmas pageant this time." And with that, she bursts into tears.

"Bad daddy! Bad daddy! *Bad daddy!*"

"Come on, kids," Robin says, scooping up the irate toddler elf. "We're all exhausted. Let's get out of these costumes, shall we?"

Tim follows his family inside. He now distinctly remembers that he did, in fact, promise to go to the Christmas pageant. He also remembers that Robin reminded him about it this morning. But then fire after fire at work drove the pageant entirely from his mind.

Tim takes off his suit jacket as his family traipses up the staircase to the second floor. Inside the vaulted foyer, Christa's chant continues to bounce off the walls.

Tim retreats to the kitchen and peers into the fridge to find a covered plate of rosemary chicken, mashed potatoes, and brussels sprouts. He pops it into the microwave, pulls a beer out of the fridge, and gulps down half of it. The microwave dings, and he wolfs down his delicious dinner without tasting it, washing it down with a second beer. Then he leans forward on his barstool and puts his head in his hands.

How did this happen?

He knows that early in his career, when they started having kids, he wasn't the best husband or the best dad. He just wasn't there much. He was learning from Bertha, trying to run and scale the business so he could create more free time. He was fired up, motivated to invest time in a business that would give his family a better life.

Once the business grew large enough and successful enough, he reasoned, he could be around more. Every time he missed a family dinner or a baseball game or a school play, he told himself things would get better. But they never seemed to. The business has only taken more and more of his time and energy. And now here he is, thirteen years into FastTrack Home Services, feeling completely lost.

He slumps forward and closes his eyes. Seemingly moments later, he feels a hand on his shoulder.

"What?" he says, jolting upright. He has fallen asleep at the counter yet again.

"You have mashed potatoes on your face," Robin says wryly.

"Hello," he says.

"Would you like to hear about the Christmas pageant?" Robin asks, crossing her arms.

"Robin," Tim says. "Look, I—"

"I don't want to hear it," she snaps. "There's always a reason. Always something that's more important than your family."

Despite his fatigue, Tim feels his hackles rise.

"Look, Robin," he says through gritted teeth. "We live in this nice house in a great school district. We can buy all the designer clothes and baseball equipment and after-school music programs we want. You drive a Lexus. You don't have to—"

"I feel like I've told you this a million times," Robin says in a quiet, broken voice. "I would much rather live in a run-down apartment and go back to work than feel like I'm raising these three kids alone. I swear, Christa barely knows who you are."

Tim finds himself on his feet, going for another beer. He pops the top and glugs down a huge mouthful as Robin watches.

Her face crumples. "I barely know who you are," she says quietly, and walks out of the room.

Tim closes his eyes and drinks the other half of the beer before stumbling into the living room as usual, making sure his alarm is set for 5:30 a.m. Among the dozens of unanswered texts, he sees a message from his college buddy and clicks on it.

"Just heard you're a 40 Under 40 honoree! Way to go, buddy! What a superstar."

Tim collapses onto the couch next to the Christmas tree and closes his eyes. In his head, his little Christmas elf's cries seem to swirl around and around as he drifts off.

Bad daddy. Bad daddy. Bad daddy.

What a superstar.

Is your business burning you out? Get resources that can help you build a business you love while enjoying your life at ScalableBusinessFramework.com.

Chapter 2

The Mentor

"Quadruple-shot extra-hot caramel macchiato, please."

It's ten thirty in the morning, and Tim is at his usual coffee joint, La Chance Café. Whenever he has meetings outside the office or needs to schedule a coffee with someone, he tries to stop here for a much-needed pick-me-up.

They have, in his opinion, the best coffee in town, and today he really needs it. He slept horribly last night, and he's been at it since early this morning.

As the barista gives Tim his total, he fishes in his pocket for his wallet. It's not there.

"No, no, *no*." He digs around in his other pocket and looks hopefully at the floor, then helplessly up at the barista, who is wearing a tiny, jaunty Santa hat.

"Well, I guess I'm going without today," he says. "Must've left my wallet at the office."

"No worries, friend," a voice says. Tim turns to see a man, perhaps in his mid-forties, with a thick shock of gray hair and a warm smile. He's holding a newspaper in one hand.

"Hiya, Barry," the barista says. "That's awfully nice of you."

"Not a problem," Barry says, stepping up to hand the barista his credit card. "I'll take the usual."

"Double shot Americano, coming right up."

As the barista scans the card and hands it back, Tim faces his unexpected benefactor. The pair are of a similar height, although Barry seems to be in much better shape than Tim.

"Thanks, man," he says. "I'm Tim. Do I know you? You look really familiar."

"No, I don't think so," Barry says, shaking Tim's hand. "But I've seen you around La Chance quite a few times. You must work nearby."

Tim looks at Barry and nods as they make their way to the pickup counter. "Yeah, that must be it. I think I see you sitting in here a lot as well. Do you work nearby too?"

"In a fashion," Barry says. "I founded Beacon Home Services down on First Street. These days I'm chairman of the board, and I just pop in when I'm in town for meetings and such."

"Oh! Yeah, Beacon is in home services like HVAC and plumbing, right? But hang on . . . you're already retired? You can't be much more than a decade older than me."

Barry laughs. "I'll take that as a compliment. I did step down from the CEO position early, but it wasn't to retire; it was to work on other projects. I'm actually fifty-five, so a little more of an age gap than you think."

"How do you know how old I am?" Tim says, conscious that he looks much older than he actually is.

Barry waves his newspaper, and Tim sees his own face staring back at him, eye bags and all. The paper is unfolded to the "40 Under 40" section.

"Oh, yeah, that," Tim says. "My phone has been blowing up all morning."

"Well, congratulations to you," Barry says. "It's quite an achievement."

"Thanks," Tim says, shrugging. "Honestly, it doesn't feel like much of one."

"What do you mean?" Barry asks.

"Barry!" the barista calls, sliding two drinks under the pickup sign. Tim grabs his, then looks at his new acquaintance.

"It's—well, it's a long story."

"I'd love to hear it when you've got the time," Barry says. He looks genuinely interested, and Tim feels a pang. Wouldn't it feel good to offload some of his stress onto another entrepreneur?

"Well, I've gotta run right now, but maybe I'll take you up on that," Tim says, looking at Barry. *There's something about this guy,* he thinks. *Maybe I could learn something from him.*

"Let's do that," Barry says. "Here, take my card."

Tim glances at the card. It's thick with a minimalistic design. Beneath Barry's name, the text reads "Founder, Charis Strategies."

"Thanks, and thanks again for the coffee, Barry," he says.

"No problem," Barry replies. "Congrats again on the '40 Under 40' list, seriously. Maybe I'll see you around."

* * *

For the next week, Tim begins to notice Barry whenever he goes into La Chance for his quadruple-shot macchiato. Barry always looks cheerful and often meets with people who, despite their casual clothing, seem to be working. He's clearly using this space as a casual meetup spot for his business consulting venture.

Tim is so curious, especially given Beacon's adjacent area of business, that he makes time one day to look up the history of both Beacon and Charis Strategies. He's flabbergasted to learn that Beacon, which was started around the same time as FastTrack Home Solutions, boasts a workforce of three hundred. It provides HVAC, plumbing, electrical, and related services for corporations—not just in the South, but on a national scale.

And then there's Barry, who transitioned the day-to-day of running Beacon to his team at forty-eight. He seems healthy, stress-free, and beloved by everyone who encounters him. Tim gleans from his online search that Charis Strategies is a small, boutique business that Barry apparently runs part-time for fun. It has a simple landing page with gushing testimonials from some very highly regarded entrepreneurs, including some prominent national business leaders. Barry might be the bolt from the blue Tim needs.

Tim walks into La Chance one Monday to find Barry at his usual table, looking as though he's getting ready to leave. After visiting the counter, Tim walks over, feeling awkward.

"Barry, hi. I'm Tim. Do you remember me from last week?"

"Sure do," Barry says. "How have you been?"

"Okay," Tim says. "Do you mind if I run something by you?"

"Not at all, Tim," Barry says, folding his hands in front of him. Today he's dressed in athletic clothing and has a gym bag next to his table. "Please, take a seat."

"I want to know how you did it," Tim blurts, plopping down in the chair opposite Barry.

Barry smiles kindly.

"That is . . . you seem to have it all together," Tim says. "You built this great business, and it's absolutely thriving, and you were able to step back from the day-to-day so early, and you just seem so happy and healthy. The point is, Barry, I wouldn't even consider FastTrack a competitor with Beacon because I'm such a small fry. I may have made that '40 Under 40' list, and I may drive a nice car and live in a nice house, but the truth is, I'm about to lose it."

Tim runs a hand through his hair in exasperation. "I want to build and scale FastTrack, but right now it's driving me nuts. I work practically nonstop, my kids barely know me, my back feels awful, and I think my wife is seriously contemplating divorce. I'm falling apart, and you aren't, and I want to know your secret."

Barry smiles and nods. "You're interested in business consulting."

"Please," says Tim. "I'm kind of desperate."

Barry thinks for a moment, then nods as if making up his mind. "We've got the holidays right around the corner," he says. "How about we start fresh in the new year?"

Tim exhales and lets out a relieved laugh. "That sounds perfect. A fresh start is exactly what I need."

Looking for your own fresh start? Get resources that can help you build a business you love while enjoying your life at ScalableBusinessFramework.com.

Part 2

The Three P's

Chapter 3

Purpose

"Good to see you again, Tim," Barry says, standing to shake his hand.

"You too, Barry. Happy New Year."

The coffee shop isn't too crowded this Tuesday afternoon, and Tim slides his seat back, trying to muster a smile. It's a chilly day, but inside it's nice and warm and smells of butter and coffee.

Even though Tim feels exhausted, as he collapses into his chair, he can't help but feel a bit of hope as he looks at his new mentor. Barry is practically glowing with health and seems to have acquired a tan over the holidays.

"Thanks again for meeting with me," Tim says. "I bought us snacks." He slides a plate of snickerdoodles onto the table along with his usual quadruple-shot macchiato.

"Oh, that was very kind of you," Barry says. "How were your holidays?"

"They ... could have been better," Tim says, pulling napkins methodically out of the napkin dispenser. "I worked way too much. Surprising, right?" He sighs, exasperated. "It just seemed like catastrophe after catastrophe, and I ended up missing a couple of holiday parties and whatnot. My wife was ... not pleased." He grimaces. "How were your holidays?"

"Well, I'm sorry to hear yours weren't so great," Barry says with a sympathetic smile. "My wife and I flew our kids out to Bermuda for a white-sand Christmas."

"That explains the tan," Tim says, trying not to sound grumpy as he puts the pile of napkins on the table in front of him and pulls his laptop out of his bag.

"Yeah, I suppose it does," Barry says. Then he leans forward, his eyes bright. "Tim, I'm not here to sugarcoat anything. I've been where you are, and I know how overwhelming it can feel. But I think our work together will change everything for you. I really do."

Tim looks at Barry's earnest expression. "I'm really hoping this mentorship helps me out," he agrees. "I just want some of your secret sauce."

Tim seizes a napkin and grabs a cookie. "Sorry, I had to skip lunch," he says, taking a huge bite and setting the rest on the napkin pile.

"No problem," Barry says, nodding. "Eat away. I've got a lot to say. Today, I'm going to outline the Three P's: purpose, people, and profit. I call my business structure the Scalable Business Framework, and we'll get to that eventually, but the Three P's are the foundation of it all. If you want to scale a business and enjoy the journey, you must first design a business you love. It starts with the Three P's."

Tim starts a new document on his laptop and takes Barry's words down, stuffing the rest of the sickly-sweet cookie into his mouth. He looks up at Barry, who has paused to look out the window at a passing elderly woman walking two cute French bulldogs.

"Are you sure you don't want a cookie?" Tim asks sheepishly, taking another one.

"Twist my arm," Barry says, taking a cookie and placing it on a napkin untouched. "Let's start with the first P—purpose. Do you know the purpose of your business, Tim?"

Tim opens his mouth to respond, then hesitates. "To, uh, provide HVAC services?" he offers. Even as he says it, he knows it sounds lame.

Barry chuckles softly. "That's a *function*, Tim, not a purpose. Here's a personal example for you. When I stepped down from Beacon and started Charis Strategies, it was because I realized that I'm really just a builder. I love building things, including businesses, for myself and for others. It's a way I can impact people both inside and outside the company. That's my purpose. Through and through, if I'm not building, I'm just like, 'Man, I'm missing out.' That is what I love."

"I can tell," Tim says, typing notes. Barry's enthusiasm practically radiates from him.

"It took me about ten years into my career to figure that out," Barry says, staring out into space. "I was always starting businesses, then stepping away once they took off. I kept thinking, 'There's something wrong with me; I keep leaving good stuff behind.' I can't tell you how many friends have taken me out to lunch and asked, 'What are you doing? That business is exploding! Why are you getting out now?'"

Tim laughs. "I could see that. People think you're crazy for wanting to start over when you already have something good going."

"Well, I'm definitely not going to leave Charis Strategies anytime soon," Barry says. "It was born out of my personal mission statement to help other people build and scale their businesses the right way. I've found my purpose, and I'm more excited and energized today than I've ever been."

"So, you found your purpose through helping other people build?"

"Yes," Barry says, the edges of his eyes crinkling with a smile. "I think it's because I'm living out my calling and my purpose. In those other businesses we created, I loved the people and most of the clients, but I wasn't really passionate about what we were doing. This is totally different. Every single day, I get to wake up and build. That's my passion. That's what I love doing. And that's why it's sustainable. I feel very blessed and fortunate to have figured that out and built a business model around it. I really do hop out of bed every morning excited to get to work." Barry laughs and makes a sweeping gesture with both hands. "I know that's not normal, and I'm very grateful for that opportunity. I love facilitating relationships that will impact millions of people's lives. I've been doing it for years, and Charis Strategies has allowed me to do it in a more effective and organized way. I love this so much that I would totally do it for free," he says with another laugh. "It's my kind of mission and business."

"I don't know if I'll ever be that passionate about FastTrack," admits Tim. Barry looks unbelievably happy just talking about his work. It's hard not to envy him.

Barry nods. "I get it, but at the same time, I had so much fun and gained so much fulfillment with my other businesses, including Beacon. You can find purpose that keeps you going in your business too, and then maybe someday you'll be ready to move on. Let's build something great on the foundation you've laid already, and then we'll see what else you can do."

"Barry, that's really great and all, and sure, I do have some emotional attachment to my business. But . . . well, it's HVAC. We have to make money. I definitely wouldn't do this for free," Tim says with a wry smile. "My question is, how do you keep from getting taken advantage of if you're just trying to fulfill some kind of higher purpose?"

Barry smiles, cradling his mug in two tanned hands. "That's a common concern. But here's the thing—when you have a clear purpose, it doesn't just guide your decisions; it shapes your entire business model. At Beacon, for example, we built our services around a purpose, and in doing so, we also built a loyal customer base that appreciates and values what we do. And yes, we're profitable. Very profitable, in fact."

"Yes, sorry," Tim says, embarrassed. "I know how successful Beacon is, and I don't mean to question you. But what *is* Beacon's purpose?"

"I'm not going to tell you," Barry says.

Tim shoots him a look, and he laughs. "Since you're in the same area of business, telling you might take away your opportunity to figure out your own purpose," Barry explains. "What I will say is that, as a leader and entrepreneur, you can build a business you love in practically any field, and building a business you love around a fulfilling purpose is the only real path to success."

Tim sits back, digesting Barry's words. "But how do you find that balance between profitability and purpose? They just don't seem compatible to me. It still kind of seems like one or the other for my particular business."

"I completely understand," Barry says, setting his mug back down. "It's crucial to find a balance between profitability, impact, and alignment with your calling and passions. Many people start businesses to make money, but they can lose sight of what truly matters and why they began in the first place. And so often this happens because we get trapped in the belief that we have to build something up to sell or exit and make a lot of money."

Tim nods, typing away.

"If you're just chasing money, you'll eventually burn out," Barry continues, holding his hands apart. "Without a sense of purpose, it's hard to keep going when things get tough. I think we often get things mixed up and backward when it comes to profit and purpose. It's all connected in my mind. If you focus on creating meaning, finding joy while on the journey, and building with excellence, you'll end up with something valuable—something with a purpose."

Barry steeples his fingers in front of him, putting his elbows on the table. "Most importantly, people are attracted to that, which ultimately leads to more profit. You could have done anything, but you started this business for a reason. It was a combination of your skills, your desires, what you care about, and who you want to serve. It might not have been intentional, but recognizing those elements and reconnecting with them will help you get started."

"Yeah, okay," Tim says, his mind starting to churn with ideas.

Barry pauses for a moment as Tim takes a few notes. When Tim looks up, Barry is holding a small piece of cookie, which he pops into his mouth.

"Delicious," he declares. "Now, Tim, I have a question for you. Have you ever heard of Viktor Frankl?"

Tim shakes his head, reaching automatically for another cookie. "No, who's that?"

"Frankl was an Austrian psychiatrist and a Jewish survivor of the Holocaust," Barry explains. "He lived through the horrors of World War II, spending time in a concentration camp and experiencing some of the worst circumstances imaginable. Yet he was able to stay resilient and survive. How do you think he managed that?"

"Honestly? I have no idea," Tim says.

"Frankl believed that everything can be taken from a person," Barry says, "except one thing: the last of human freedoms—to choose one's attitude in any given set of circumstances, to choose one's own way."

"That's... humbling," Tim says. "My life seems overwhelming sometimes, but if he could do it, I suppose I should be able to as well."

Barry nods. "It's a real demonstration of human resilience. After the war, Frankl devoted his life to helping people with severe depression and those who had gone through traumatic experiences. He developed a school of psychotherapy called logotherapy. It's centered on the idea that the primary human drive is the search for meaning and purpose, not the pursuit of pleasure or other external factors. Put simply, when you're living out your purpose, when your life has meaning, you'll be happy and content and lead a fulfilling life."

Tim leans back, processing this. "So, he believed that finding meaning and purpose was more important than just enjoying life?"

"Exactly," Barry says, giving the table an emphatic pat. "Frankl's perspective was radical at the time. While others believed happiness came from pleasure, Frankl knew from his own suffering that you can't always control your circumstances. Life can be incredibly hard, but even in the worst situations, you can find happiness and contentment by living out your purpose. If you're not living your purpose, pleasures are just a way to numb the pain. I should mention that this approach worked even on Frankl's incredibly traumatized patients. None of his patients ever committed suicide, even though people with severe trauma have relatively high suicide rates."[1]

Tim takes a few notes, then sits back in his chair with his drink. "That . . . that kind of blows my mind," he says. "Here I am feeling sorry for myself, but nothing I've gone through can compare to any of that. So, it's about choosing your attitude and finding purpose to fuel your success."

"I don't think you need to disparage your own situation, but it certainly helps to reframe things," Barry says, pausing to wave at someone at the front of the store. Tim turns to see a well-dressed woman bustling out, coffee in hand, giving Barry a cheery wave.

"For me, finding your purpose and serving others isn't about what you do, but who you are," Barry says. "It's about aligning your work with your true self, so even when things get tough, you have the resilience to keep going. That's why a solid business model starts with a higher purpose. It's essential to have a greater mission beyond just the day-to-day operations."

---

1   Viktor Frankl, *Man's Search for Meaning* (Beacon Press, 1959).

Barry pauses, playing with a small piece of cookie. "As a business owner who has made a lot of mistakes and learned a lot of lessons, I feel uniquely qualified and have a ton of empathy for other business leaders trying to do the same thing. We really try to be that business that helps put the right disciplines, processes, and systems in place to help them scale and grow the right way." He sets down the cookie fragment and starts ticking off talking points on his fingers. "It's about building personal relationships, understanding that clients are people just like you, and showing empathy. It's about helping them identify pain points they may not even realize are affecting their business, customers, or employees. It's about being a blessing."

"Blessing people with HVAC," Tim mutters.

Barry laughs. "Maybe. I have a worksheet for you to fill out to help you identify FastTrack's purpose. For me, just know that having the ability to be a blessing, to help businesses and relationships grow, and to integrate my personal beliefs into my professional life has been a game-changer."

Tim leans back, swallowing the last of his cookie. "So, it's not just about making money—it's about making a difference. And if you do that right, the money follows. It's not about either money or purpose—it's about the partnership of both."

Barry nods. "You've got it. Having that mission, that higher purpose, gives you the durability to weather any storm. There are many external factors—like the economy, pandemics, and interest rates—that we can't control. My job is to build a business that thrives regardless of those circumstances."

Tim's eyes narrow as he considers this. "But how do you do that? How do you make sure your business survives the storm?"

"By focusing on what we can control, which is a strong foundation," Barry says, his tone firm. "There will be seasons when things go better and seasons when they're tougher due to those external factors. But I firmly believe that if you have a strong foundation built on purpose, focus on what you can control, get better every day, and improve your business, you'll create opportunities for the future no matter the economic situation."

Tim nods, typing. "So, purpose is part of a strong foundation."

"Exactly," Barry says. "Companies that are built the right way around a purpose, with solid systems and processes and decisions based on data rather than feelings, will be in a position to seize those opportunities. You need all those elements, but it starts with purpose. It's really about keeping your head down and doing the right thing—planting the right seeds so you produce the right results in the right season. That's what we advise our clients to do, and it's exactly how I built Beacon to be so successful."

Tim nods. "So purpose is a big ingredient in that secret sauce I asked you about."

Barry nods, his eyes gleaming with conviction. "Oh, yes. Purpose helps you focus on what you can control and stay committed to who you want to become as a company. Don't let circumstances dictate those decisions. You need to decide ahead of time who you want to be and stick to that. That mindset gives you the freedom to say no when you need to."

Tim takes a deep breath. He's been so busy treading water day-to-day that he forgot to consider the full picture. For the first time, he feels like he has the tools to do just that.

"Thanks, Barry," Tim says, taking a big sip of his now-tepid drink, his voice steady. "I think I'm ready to start. But what do I do first? How do I figure out my purpose?"

"I'm going to give you two homework assignments," Barry says. "First, I brought you this."

He reaches into his gym bag, pulls out a battered copy of a book, and hands it to Tim. Tim glances at the cover: *Beyond Entrepreneurship 2.0* by Jim Collins.

"Have you ever heard of this book?" Barry asks Tim.

"No," Tim says. He hasn't had time to read anything but emails in years.

"This is a prerequisite for my mentees," Barry says. "It's a masterclass that walks through some of Jim Collins's best teachings. Jim has spent his career studying businesses that have grown and outlasted their competitors. The topics are foundational for every great leader and include insight on leadership, strategy, innovation, and tactical excellence. I want to give it to you now because it's very enmeshed in the concept of purpose, although what Collins talks about here is vision, which is a little broader."

"Vision?" Tim asks.

"Yes," Barry says. "You'll need to read the book so we can really dig into this, but the gist is that vision is the unification of core values, purpose, and an envisioned future. Purpose is a huge piece of that. Take values and add purpose and the future you'd like to have, and you get your vision."

"Okay, I'll somehow fit this into my schedule," Tim says with a laugh. "I'm not a fast reader."

"You could try the audiobook version," Barry says. "You just need to get it into your brain within the next three weeks. But for next week, I just need you to read section 4, which is all about values."

"Got it," Tim says, slipping the book into his bag as Barry pulls out his phone.

"I emailed you the second piece of homework," Barry says. "It's a worksheet I've designed that I use with many of my clients."

Tim switches to his inbox, opens the worksheet, and scans its contents. "This is really comprehensive."

Barry nods. "I designed it to help you really think about why you're in this business in the first place. What do you care about? What do you want your legacy to be? Once you have that, the rest will come. And I'll be here to help you along the way."

Tim nods.

"I've broken the worksheet down into a series of questions to help you reflect on your purpose—from both internal and external perspectives," Barry says. "Please make sure to fill it out before our next meeting. We can go over it together then."

"That's going to be a lot of work," Tim says, mostly to himself.

"It is, but it'll give you clarity," Barry insists. "The more time you spend reflecting on these questions, the clearer your purpose will become. And once you've got that, everything else—your decisions, your business model—will align with what really matters to you."

Tim looks up at Barry and nods. "I see how this will help. I'll print this out and get started on it."

Barry smiles. "Good. Really take your time with it."

Tim writes down a reminder for himself, feeling a flicker of hope inside. For the first time in a long while, he's not just thinking about getting through the next day.

"Thank you, Barry," he says, standing and sliding his laptop back into his bag. "Same time next week?"

"Same time next week," Barry agrees wholeheartedly, shaking Tim's hand. Tim slips his coat on and walks out into the cool, cloudy day feeling a little brighter.

Chapter 3 Summary

Introduction to the Three P's—Purpose

The Three P's
- **Purpose**: The main motivation behind long-term success and business sustainability.
- **People**: A focus on building and supporting a strong team based on purpose.
- **Profit**: A byproduct of aligning business with purpose and getting your team on board.

Purpose, Values, and Vision
- **Purpose Beyond Services**: Scaling a business requires a purpose beyond just delivering a product or service.
- **Values:** Core beliefs that shape your purpose, which ensures clarity in decision-making and long-term fulfillment.
- **Vision**: Values + purpose + your envisioned future = vision.

Purpose Worksheet

*All people end up somewhere in life,
but few end up there on purpose.*
—**Craig Groeschel**[2]

Everything starts with your purpose. Your purpose is your driving force that undergirds your efforts and unites your skills and passion. Understanding your purpose is critical to building a business you love that is aligned with that purpose. Unpack this through the self-assessment steps below.

What Is Your Purpose? (Fill this out last)

> *Peace. We deliver peace of mind to our customers when key systems in their home aren't working efficiently and effectively. We take away the chaos, worry, and stress.*

---

[2] Craig Groeschel, "Chazown," Life.Church, July 18, 2011, https://www.life.church/media/chazown/chazown/.

Internal Assessment

Part 1: Self-Reflection

What are some things you love doing (that don't feel like work and give you energy and joy)?

> I love serving and helping customers. When we arrive at a customer's home, they're often stressed and worried about the complexity and cost of the repair. I love putting their minds at ease by treating them the way we'd want one of our own relatives to be treated. It's incredibly fulfilling to solve their problem at a fair price. The real joy comes from seeing their stress and worry melt away. We take pride in being a small light of hope and joy in their lives.

What talents or skills come naturally to you (things that feel easy for you but may be challenging for others)?

- I'm empathetic to our customers. What we do is really hard and challenging. Something inside me is driven to help our customers and mentor our team to better serve them.

- Diagnosing the problems our customers are having. I can usually figure out the problem without seeing the system based only on the description they give over the phone. It almost feels like a superpower, but this isn't really my job—it's my sales team's job.

- Coming up with multiple solutions so the customer can pick the best option for them. I'm really good at laying out the pros/cons of each option so they can make a wise decision.

What other things give you energy?
Solving our customers' problems and seeing them get their joy back.

What zaps your energy?
All the administrative tasks of running a business. I like helping customers, not doing accounting, creating SOPs, dealing with customer complaints, handling HR issues, etc. I want to help serve our customers, not put out fires all day long and deal with all the administrative issues. It seems like I can never work <u>on</u> the business because I'm constantly working <u>in</u> the business.

When was one time in your life when you felt you were firing on all cylinders? Who were the people involved? What was your role, and how did your actions impact them?
It was definitely in the early days of the business, when I was doing the work and serving the customers. It felt like I was "in the zone"—I loved solving the problems and bringing peace of mind to our customers.

Take an inventory of your answers above. What patterns and commonalities do you see?

> I rely on my intuition a lot. I'm good at what I do but don't always understand why. I also pride myself on working harder than everyone else. Nobody ever out-works me. I also get energy from solving other people's issues so they can live peacefully.

Part 2: Finding Your Purpose

Write down your story. How do your experiences make you uniquely qualified to help others in a certain area?

> My mom raised me on her own, and money was always tight. Things were constantly breaking around the house, and my mom had no one to call for help. Our air conditioner went out during a heat wave one summer, and Bertha came right over and even gave my mom a discount and a payment plan that actually worked for us.
>
> That kindness really stuck with me. It made me admire Bertha as a business owner. Looking back, I realize that's when I knew I wanted to build a business that helped families like mine. I have the unique qualification of understanding what it's like to be on the other side of the interaction, and I have the empathy and understanding to help meet customers where they are.

What problems/challenges excite you?

I love coming into a situation in a home where the customer is really concerned and stressed about the system not working (and how much it's going to cost). It's so fulfilling to find ways to fix the problem and restore peace to the customer. There's no drug on earth that can make me feel the way I do when one of our customers is happy with the work we've done.

Of the problems/challenges that excite you, what businesses or business models exist that you can improve upon and do better?

Because of our passion for serving homeowners and my personal experiences growing up with a single mom who didn't have a lot of extra money, we're uniquely empathetic to the needs of our customers. It's personal to us, while it's often just transactional to our competition. We also have a lot of experience and expertise offering alternative solutions that give our customers options. Not everyone can afford to replace their systems. We always try to recommend multiple options so the customer doesn't feel pressured to do something that isn't right for them.

In what areas do your talents, passions, and opportunities to build a real business intersect?

We can really make a difference for people by giving them options, being transparent, working quickly, and getting it right the first time so that we don't waste our clients' money and time. We've developed a way to serve our ideal customers and make money on each job (or at least we used to when I was doing most of the work). We've struggled lately as our team hasn't been able to do things as consistently as I did in the early days.

External Assessment

If you overheard these groups talking about you to each other, what would you hope they would say?

Your family:
The best husband and father in the world

Your friends:
Successful and loyal

Your team:
Servant leader, the hardest worker in the company

Your customers:
Empathetic, truly care about me and my home

Capture the commonalities from these and distill out your core values. What are they?

Loyalty, servant leadership, empathy, relationships, success

Ask those close to you, whom you trust and respect, about your unique abilities and passions. Capture those and compare them with your own observations. What overlaps are there?

I'm too scared to do this! I don't think I'll like the answers they'd give at this point in my life. There's a huge gap between where I am today and where I want to be. They would probably agree that I'm a hard worker and loyal, and most people consider me successful from a business standpoint. But I work all the time and don't focus on these important relationships anymore.

I'm not a very good husband, father, and friend right now.

Values and Vision Statement

What do you value as a person?

Respect. I want to be respected by my family and my teammates. I also want customers to love us and the work we do for them.

For your ideal job, describe the work environment that makes it attractive to you. What core values define this job?

I love to work and enjoy working hard. But I don't want to be in an environment that's chaotic and reactive. I love being in control and helping people. I don't enjoy helping people who don't appreciate me and what I do. I do love helping people where I can truly make a difference in their life.

Based on these questions and the rest of this worksheet, what are your core values?

- *Serving and helping customers as if they are family*

- *Educating customers on the pros/cons of solutions so they can pick the right one for them based on their needs and budget*

- *No shortcuts—we only do things the right way*

Now, from those values, formulate a vision statement.

To better everyone around me by serving them.

Learn more about purpose and download a blank, printable version of this worksheet at ScalableBusinessFramework.com.

Chapter 4

Leadership

The large window beside Barry lets in the soft afternoon light, casting a warm glow across the café. Tim settles into his chair, coffee cup in one hand, a paper bag clutched in the other. He feels a sense of anticipation. The previous discussion on purpose has already catalyzed a change for him.

Barry sits back in his chair, smiling at Tim. He's wearing his usual activewear. "How are you today?" he asks.

"I'm doing a little better, actually," Tim says. "How are you?"

"Great," Barry says. "Actually, I've been meaning to tell you that I will be out of town next week. I'm running a marathon."

"Of course you are."

Barry shrugs, smiling. "Do you want to continue our meetings virtually during that time, or would you rather take a break?"

"Let's continue online," Tim says. "I don't want to lose momentum. By the way, my wife sent along a treat with me today." He draws a few muffins out of the paper bag and sets them on a napkin.

"Bran and cran, low fat. I told her you're a health nut. Would you believe I've been at home by seven every day except one since our last meeting? She wanted to say thanks."

Barry laughs heartily and takes a muffin. "Please tell Robin thank you for me," he says, then takes a bite. "What inspired the change?"

"That worksheet you gave me." Tim pulls the battered pages out of his laptop sleeve, wincing as he spots a few grease stains. "Doing it by hand helps me think," he says with a self-deprecating grin.

"Oh, this is delightful," Barry says in a muffled voice, his eyes lighting up as he bites into the muffin. He doesn't seem to mind Tim's grease-stained worksheet.

"Well, I've got a whole bunch of them for you right here," Tim says, setting the paper bag of muffins atop Barry's gym duffel and snagging a bite himself. Robin, who had handed him the bag this morning with a genuine smile, seems a little happier now that he's been making it home for dinner every night, even though he's had to pull out his laptop a few times in the evenings. He has even been free to help put the kids to bed a few times, although the first time,

Christa screamed bloody murder when he tried to give her a bath. It stung Tim to realize he wasn't part of her routine anymore.

"Much obliged," Barry says. "Now, let's get started. Were you able to identify your purpose?"

Tim spreads the pages of the worksheet on the table so they're facing Barry. Barry leans over and looks at the top of the first page.

"Peace," Barry says. "What a lovely purpose."

"When a customer's home system isn't working, it creates chaos and stress," Tim explains. "I think solving their problems and restoring their peace of mind is my purpose."

"That's beautiful," Barry says proudly. "How did you arrive at that?"

"Well, once I dug through all the surface-level stuff, I actually realized that it all started with my mom," Tim says.

"Oh?" Barry says.

"Yeah," Tim says. "She raised me by herself, and money was tight. Stuff was always breaking around the house—the oven, the toilet—and she had nowhere to turn. When Bertha started her company, she was so quick to step in and help out when the air conditioner went out one really hot summer." Tim smiles as he remembers. "She even gave my mom a discount and a really doable payment plan."

"That must have been life-changing," Barry says.

"It was. There was a heat wave that summer, and before Bertha stepped in, we were sleeping in puddles of our own sweat. It really saved the day."

"Alabama summers can be brutal," Barry says sympathetically.

"Don't we know it." Tim's smile fades as he remembers. "That kind act really stuck with me," he says. "It's what made me admire Bertha so much as a business owner. I realized I wanted to build a business that served homeowners like my mom—people who deserved peace of mind at a price they could afford."

He meets Barry's eyes, nodding to himself. "That became the purpose of the business for me, even though I didn't know it. And that purpose drove everything Bertha and I did at first. Then I lost sight of it along the way somehow." He lets out a sigh, resting his chin in his hand. "I've been so focused on just making things work that I haven't really thought about the bigger picture in years."

Barry quietly sips his coffee, waiting. Tim runs a hand through his hair, looking at the upside-down worksheet and gathering his thoughts.

"There's this huge gap between who I am now and who I want to be," Tim says finally. "I want my family to see me as the best husband and father, and there's no way they do right now because it's just not true. That's why I've already started making some changes, like actually coming home for dinner even if it feels like FastTrack is about to explode. But that's just a baby step. I'm not the husband, father, or friend I want to be. People know I'm a hard worker and see me as successful, but there's a lot I need to fix."

Barry pounds the table lightly with one fist. "Tim, recognizing that gap is crucial," he says. "You've identified a wonderful purpose, and there's no need to beat yourself up. It's amazing that you've already decided to take action and make some changes to your personal life. Remember to celebrate your wins, even if they feel small."

Tim nods morosely.

"Now it's time to move forward, and to do that, we need to talk about vision," Barry says, clapping his hands. "Did you read the vision section of *Beyond Entrepreneurship 2.0*?"

"I did!" Tim says. "Well, I listened to the audiobook version during my commute. I really liked it, actually."

"Great," Barry says. "Do you remember what makes a good vision according to Collins?

"I think I wrote that down in my notes somewhere." Tim opens his laptop. "Hang on." He starts scrolling until he finds what he's looking for.

What Makes a Great Vision

- Rooted in values: Reflects the organization's core values and purpose

- Ambitious and inspiring: Sets challenging goals that motivate and excite

- Clearly articulated: Communicated in a clear and compelling way

- Aligned with action: The organization's actions and decisions have to be consistent with its vision[3]

Tim rattles this off to Barry, feeling a little like a student vying for a good grade.

"That's right," Barry says. "And did you think at all about *your* vision? To do that, you first had to pinpoint your values."

"Yes," Tim says, flipping to the right page of the worksheet. "My vision is to be dedicated to the service and success of everyone around me. That's based on my core value of respect. I want to be respected by my family and my teammates, and I want customers to love us and the work we do for them."

"Excellent," Barry says. "And do you feel your vision aligns with the way you're currently running your business?"

"Absolutely not," Tim says, making a face. "My real values are in service and helping others, but I've been sucked into this method of trying to help myself first. I think it's about the business, but the business is really just me. I don't act empathetically toward my team; I just care about their output. I love my family, but sometimes I see them as a burden keeping me from what really matters. I've got it all flipped upside down!" He flings his hands into the air in exasperation, nearly upsetting his coffee cup in the process.

---

3   James C. Collins and Bill Lazier, *Beyond Entrepreneurship 2.0: Turning Your Business into an Enduring Great Company* (Random House, 2020), 34–36.

"Realizing that is a huge step in the right direction," Barry says as Tim steadies his cup. "You can use this realization to reset things in both your personal and professional lives. Be transparent about the changes you're making, and start to evaluate your business culture and determine what doesn't measure up. Take note of activities or messaging that runs counter to your purpose."

"Can do," Tim says, typing this into his notes. "That's a good idea." He sits back for a moment, cup in hand. "I don't think I wrote this down exactly, but I really liked what Collins said about the effect a vision has on the team. He mentioned that by laying out a vision that embodies core values and long-term goals, leaders can inspire their teams to achieve exceptional and enduring results. That sounds like a recipe for success to me."

"Hey, thanks for the segue." Barry chuckles. "That's today's topic—people. At the end of the day, they're the only thing that really matters in life."

Tim creates a new heading in his notes as Barry continues to explain.

"Your business needs to stay focused on creating an intentional culture that outlines your core values," Barry says. "At Charis Strategies and the businesses we work with, our approach to people is nonnegotiable. We care about everyone—our team members, the people we serve, our partners, and anyone we come into contact with." He places his hands together, palms down, then spreads them broadly apart to emphasize the point. "If we're not taking care of people, nothing else matters."

"Hmm," Tim says, typing a few lines.

"This idea is at the core of how I run my business and how I encourage other business owners to run theirs," Barry says. "I think it's something every leader needs to understand. I can see you feel the same way, especially about your customers."

"That's true," Tim says.

"When I say 'people,' I do mean your customers," Barry says. "But I also mean your team and yourself. That's the part I want to focus on today—you and your leadership. I'm not sure you've given that part of the equation much thought."

"Oh," Tim says. "Uh, no, you're right. I really haven't."

"Do you currently have any thoughts about how you approach your team as a leader?" Barry asks.

"Um . . ."

"That's okay," Barry says, the corners of his eyes crinkling. "That's the response I usually get from business owners. First, to get your mental juices flowing, I want to read you some of my favorite quotes. There are a lot of great quotes about leadership, but let's kick things off with three of them."

Barry pulls out his phone and touches the screen a few times.

"The first one is, 'Everything rises and falls on leadership,'[4] he says. "That's author and pastor John Maxwell. I like that idea because leaders determine the direction of the organization and galvanize the team around it."

"That's true," Tim says, typing.

"The second is Bill Hybels," Barry continues. "He's actually also an author and pastor. He says, 'When the leader gets better, everyone gets better.'[5] It's the idea that when you're a business leader, you have the power to make a significant impact. You're the captain of the ship, and you have the power to turn things around."

"Easier said than done," Tim says dryly, typing the rest of the quote.

"Don't I know it," Barry says kindly. "But remember—you're not alone. There are people out there who want to help you, who want to partner with you to enhance your business and see you succeed. I'm one of those people, and there are many others like me. Even when things seem out of control, you have a vast circle of influence. Just one step can lead to a massive impact."

"Thanks," Tim says, feeling a bit better. "What's the third quote?"

"The measure of a leader is not the number of people who serve him, but the number of people he serves,"[6] Barry

---

[4] John C. Maxwell, *The 21 Irrefutable Laws of Leadership: Follow Them and People Will Follow You* (Thomas Nelson, 1998).

[5] Bill Hybels, "When the Leader Gets Better, Everyone Gets Better," speech, Global Leadership Summit, Willow Creek Community Church, August 8–9, 2013.

[6] John C. Maxwell, *The 21 Indispensable Qualities of a Leader: Becoming the Person Others Will Want to Follow* (HarperCollins Leadership, 2007).

recites. "That's Maxwell again on real leadership—*servant* leadership. To truly lead, you have to serve others and help them grow. Otherwise you're just a dictator, and nobody wants to follow a dictator."

Tim frowns. "Oops."

Barry chuckles. "When you're just trying to keep your head above water, it's easy to start barking orders without really thinking about the impact they'll have. I know that all too well. For example, as a leader, I have a natural tendency to tell people what to do rather than ask questions to really understand. It's something I've had to work on."

"That's surprising," Tim says. "Here I thought you were perfect."

Barry laughs heartily. "I'm far from perfect," he insists. "We have more in common than you know."

"Okay, well, I'll take that as a compliment," Tim says, also laughing a little. "How did you learn to tweak your leadership style?"

"Have you ever heard of Bob Tiede?" Barry asks.

"No," Tim says. "It seems like you read a lot, Barry."

"I do." Barry bends down and rummages around in his bag for a moment, then emerges with a battered book. He slides it over to Tim, who is eating another muffin.

"Tiede is an author I highly recommend, especially when it comes to asking good questions," Barry says. "You can have my copy of *Now That's a Great Question*.[7] Like most of his books, this one is completely question-based."

"As in, it's just a bunch of questions?" Tim asks. "Something to get you to think?"

"Yes," Barry says. "It's a fantastic book that helps leaders shift from barking orders to asking questions, which is true leadership. Leaders then develop their team, which is something you could benefit from. If you're anything like me, there's always room for improvement in servant leadership, and this book really helps give a different perspective."

"Thanks," Tim says, taking the book. "I'll try to read it over the next few weeks or so."

"Excellent. Tiede's ideas are a game-changer in my opinion," Barry says, breaking off another chunk of muffin. "That was one thing that really helped me shift my thought process as a leader. Another was Liz Wiseman's book *Multipliers: How the Best Leaders Make Everyone Smarter*."

"Another book?" Tim says in disbelief.

"Yes, yes, another book. Reading is great!" Barry grins. "Anyway, Wiseman came up with a great concept about two types of leaders: diminishers and multipliers. Let's talk about those a little. They represent very different leadership styles."[8]

Tim takes another bite of muffin, enjoying the tangy cranberries mingled with the spices Robin used. He writes

---

[7] Bob Tiede, *Now That's a Great Question: How to Lead with Questions to Build Relationships and Get Results* (self-published, 2020).

[8] Liz Wiseman and Greg McKeown, *Multipliers: How the Best Leaders Make Everyone Smarter* (HarperCollins, 2010).

Diminishers and *Multipliers* down in his notes and sits poised to write more, relieved that he might not have to actually read this book.

"Diminishers tell, while multipliers ask," Barry says. "Diminishers solve the problem for you, but multipliers let you solve it yourself. Diminishers focus on how your idea could have been better, while multipliers celebrate your idea. And most importantly, diminishers give you responsibility without authority, while multipliers give you both responsibility and authority."

Tim has created two columns in his notes and is typing furiously when Barry asks, "Tim, are you a diminisher or a multiplier?"

This stops him in his tracks, and he feels a cold sensation in the pit of his stomach. He looks up at Barry. "A gentleman never tells," he says finally.

Barry lets out a hoot of laughter.

"I'm not saying any of this to put you on the spot at all," Barry says. "It's just that most business owners stumble into their leadership roles, and then they have to learn about leadership retroactively."

"Yeah," Tim says ruefully. "I know the feeling."

"So, back to diminishers and multipliers for a second," Barry says. "Diminishers limit growth, while multipliers empower it. Diminishers often lack self-awareness, while multipliers have a lot of it. Diminishers don't realize how helping too much can actually hold their team back. On the other hand, multipliers know how to inspire their team to rise to the challenge. Diminishers create followers, but multipliers develop leaders."

Tim looks over what he's typed.

Diminishers	Multipliers
Tell	Ask
Solve the problem for you	Let you solve it yourself
Focus on how your idea could have been better	Celebrate your idea
Give you responsibility without authority	Give you both responsibility and authority
Limit growth	Empower growth
Lack self-awareness	High level of self-awareness
Don't realize how their over-helpfulness can hold their team back	Know how to inspire their team to rise to the challenge
Create followers	Develop leaders

Barry picks up his last bite of muffin. "The older I get and the more I lead, the more I focus on multiplying. How can I multiply people? How can I multiply impact? How can I help others achieve far more than I ever imagined? That's what true leadership is all about."

Tim finishes typing and takes a long sip of coffee, draining his cup. "Barry, this is ... this is going to be a huge adjustment for me," he says. "And you're actually making me want to read another book, or at least listen to it."

"Excellent," Barry says, thumbing muffin crumbs off his napkin as a gaggle of parents with little kids pushes past to the bathrooms. "At the end of the day, it's about the people you impact, not the degrees you earned, the projects you completed, or the money you made. Those things are important, but they're not what really counts."

Barry leans his face on his hand, gazing out the window into the afternoon. A shaft of sunlight illuminates the side of his face. "I've come to learn that healthy people help others, and hurting people—people who are in pain—hurt others," he says. "To be a great leader, you've got to focus on personal growth, getting better and prioritizing the things that matter over the tasks that might bring short-term satisfaction."

Tim mulls this over.

"Now, I do have one more leadership topic I'd like to discuss with you today: radical candor," Barry says, turning back to Tim. "This comes from Kim Scott's book *Radical Candor: Be a Kick-Ass Boss Without Losing Your Humanity*."[9]

---

9 Kim Scott, *Radical Candor: Be a Kick-Ass Boss Without Losing Your Humanity* (New York: St. Martin's Press, 2017).

"What a title," Tim says, quickly starting a new heading in his document. "I guess I need to get used to the steady stream of book references?"

"It wouldn't hurt," Barry says, his eyes sparkling.

"So, is radical candor just being really honest? Because I can do that," Tim says.

Barry laughs. "Sometimes. Scott identified four quadrants of leadership. Let me show you," he says, pulling up a diagram on his phone.

	→ Challenging Directly →	
Caring Personally ↑	**Ruinous empathy** Caring a lot but not challenging people enough	**Radical candor** Caring personally while challenging directly
	Manipulative insincerity Neither caring nor challenging	**Obnoxious aggression** Challenging directly without caring enough[10]

"According to her, the opposite of radical candor is 'ruinous empathy'—meaning you care a lot but don't challenge people enough."

"I don't think I have that issue," Tim says dryly.

"Maybe not, but it's important to be aware of it so you don't overcorrect," Barry says. "As a leader, I certainly get

---
10   Wiseman and McKeown, *Multipliers*.

caught sugarcoating things sometimes, glossing over issues with a 'Yeah, everything's fine' attitude."

Tim nods. "Okay, yes, I've definitely seen that happen."

Barry continues, "Radical candor is all about caring personally while challenging directly. It's a balance every leader needs to find. I tend to lean toward challenging directly, but I'm also not a ruinous empathy person by nature. I've actually crossed into the obnoxious aggression quadrant at times."

Tim laughs. "That sounds more familiar. But you just don't seem like the obnoxious aggression type."

"Who would've thought, right?" Barry says with a grin. "It's easy to slip into one of the other quadrants. But you and I probably only skim the surface of that one. Can you think of someone you've worked with who might fit that description?"

Tim taps his finger on his lips as he thinks. "Years ago, we had a brilliant guy at FastTrack—super smart, lots of great ideas. But he didn't care personally about anyone. I remember one time, when I was new to the business, I heard the door to this guy's office open, then heard him stomping over. He stopped at my desk and yelled, 'Stop screwing up!'—except with much stronger language, if you know what I mean."

Barry frowns.

"The weirdest part is, I had no idea what I had done wrong!" Tim says with a laugh. "To this day, I still don't know. But I absolutely remember how it felt."

"That sounds brutal," Barry says.

"Well, it was the last straw for Bertha," Tim says. "She fired him on the spot. And I can tell you I don't go around cursing at my staff, at least. I'm not stupid enough to do that."

"Of course not," Barry says. "That's an extreme example, but it's not the only problematic quadrant. Take the fourth quadrant Scott identifies: manipulative insincerity. This one's a bit more subtle. Imagine that my friend has spinach in her teeth. I don't say anything to her, but later I think, 'She looks silly with spinach in her teeth.' In that moment, I don't care enough to tell her, and I'm not challenging her directly—that's the worst quadrant, where you care the least and don't speak up."

Tim nods, typing. He pauses and takes in the quadrants as the same parents and children from earlier shove their way past the table again, the father offering a look of apology as he hurries after his wayward toddler.

"Now, Tim, it's pretty clear which quadrant we *want* to be in," Barry says. "We want to help people grow by embracing radical candor. To help you get into that quadrant, I want to walk you through my model for using radical candor effectively and giving constructive feedback. This is where Scott and I diverge. She has her own four-part model called the CARE Model, but mine is based completely on feedback."

Tim nods and starts a numbered list for himself. "Okay. Ready when you are, chief."

"The first step is getting feedback," Barry explains, then looks up. A tall, thin server has appeared next to the table, bearing a tray.

"Harper wanted you two to try the new praline latte," the server says, sliding two new mugs onto the table and collecting the empty ones. "On the house. They're made with stevia and oat milk."

"Wow, thanks, Harper!" Barry says brightly, waving at a unicorn-haired barista at the counter. "And thank you, Jim," he says to the server, who grins and nods.

"Hey, the two of you look a lot alike," Jim says. "Is this your son, Barry?"

"Nope," Barry says. "But he is a pretty cool guy."

"Thanks," Tim says as Jim makes his exit. "I'll take that as a compliment. You're in much better shape than I am."

Barry shrugs. "Well, I am running a marathon next week. Wanna join?"

"Absolutely not," Tim says, laughing and taking a sip of the foamy latte. It's surprisingly delicious. "Sounds like Harper knows you pretty well," he says.

Barry smiles with satisfaction and wipes foam from his upper lip. "What can I say? I'm predictable. Anyway, back to the first step: getting feedback."

"Getting? Not giving?"

"Getting," Barry affirms.

"I don't like the sound of that."

Barry snorts. "Yes, well, it's crucial because it builds trust," he says, cradling the hot mug. "Before you can give feedback and expect someone to accept it, you need to be open to receiving it yourself. Leaders go first."

"I guess that makes sense," Tim says reluctantly.

"You'll see—it really works," Barry says. "And the best way to get feedback is by asking for it. People aren't always going to volunteer their thoughts on how you can improve, though some might. As a leader, you have to model this behavior regularly. For example, after an important client meeting involving multiple people, jump into a debrief and ask, 'What's one thing I could have done better or differently?' Then really take that feedback in."

Tim sipped his latte, enjoying the strong, nutty flavor. "Okay, but I can see my team clamming up if I do that. They'd think it was a trap. What if people don't have anything to say?"

Barry chuckles. "Sometimes when you ask for feedback, you'll get silence. It happens, especially in one-on-ones. You ask, 'What can I do better?' and they respond with, 'I don't really know right now.'"

"Yeah, that's what I'm anticipating," Tim says. "So, how do you get out of that loop?"

"When that happens, try asking, 'What can I *stop* doing? Is there anything I'm doing right now that's getting in your way?'" Barry suggests. "That usually opens up more specific feedback. And when you ask, embrace the discomfort. Wait for the response, even if it takes a few awkward seconds. Those moments of silence can be the difference between getting valuable feedback and getting nothing at all."

Tim nods, typing notes. "And what do you do with the feedback once you get it?"

"When you receive feedback, listen with the intent to understand," Barry says. "Stephen Covey uses the analogy of an iceberg[11]: what people say is just the tip. Their true intentions lie beneath the surface. People can sense whether your intention is genuine, so it's important to really listen and apply the feedback. And when someone gives you feedback, thank them."

"Thank them?" Tim says, making a face.

"Yes!" Barry exclaims. "For example, if someone points out that you tend to interrupt during meetings, thank them for bringing it up and ask them to nudge you if they notice it again. This creates an environment of psychological safety, which is essential for building trust."

Tim sighs. "That sounds humbling."

"It is, and that's why it creates a positive feedback loop," Barry says animatedly. "And once we've built trust by getting feedback, we can move on to giving it."

"I like that a lot better," Tim says. Barry chuckles.

"It's easier to dish it out than to take it, for sure," Barry agrees. "When giving feedback, it's all about caring personally and challenging directly. But if something makes you uncomfortable, it's probably exactly what you need to

---

11 Stephen R. Covey, *The Seven Habits of Highly Effective People* (G.K. Hall, 1997).

lean into. The same goes for giving feedback. If there's a conversation you're dreading because it feels uncomfortable, it's probably a conversation that needs to happen."

Tim nods. "Yes, okay, fine. What about the feedback itself, though? I have a feeling I haven't been doing a great job at this."

"The SBI Model provides a good framework, in my opinion," Barry says.

"The what?" Tim asks.

"Situation-Behavior-Impact Model," Barry clarifies. It was created by two doctors—an organizational psychologist and a business management professor. They developed this model to reduce misunderstandings and defensiveness during feedback conversations."[12]

"Oh," Tim says. "That sounds promising."

"It works wonders," Barry says. "First, we've got a situation," he says, ticking off the steps on his fingers. "That's when you describe the situation you're in. Then you talk about the behavior you observed. Finally, you explain the impact that behavior had. For example, let's say someone interrupts their coworker during a meeting. Afterward, you could say, 'During yesterday's meeting, I noticed you interrupted others a few times. It made it hard for everyone to contribute.' Framing feedback this way makes it easier for the person to understand what needs to change and why."

---

[12] Bill Gentry and Stephen Young, "Use Situation-Behavior-Impact (SBI) to Understand Intent," Center for Creative Leadership, November 18, 2022, https://www.ccl.org/articles/leading-effectively-articles/closing-the-gap-between-intent-vs-impact-sbii.

Tim nods, finding the framework practical. "I like that. It's clear and direct."

Barry smiles. "Specificity is key. For example, instead of saying, 'Your presentation wasn't good,' you could say, 'Your presentation could be improved by adding more visuals to engage the audience.' That gives them something actionable to work on."

"Sure," Tim says. "I like that."

"Also, focus on behavior, not personality," Barry says. "Instead of saying, 'You're disorganized,' say, 'I noticed you missed a deadline. Let's work on some strategies to manage your time more effectively.' That way, the feedback is constructive and helps the person grow."

Tim jots down notes. "Okay, yeah. You're saying you noticed the issue, but the issue is the issue—the person is not the issue."

"Right," Barry says. "Gosh, this latte really is something. Gets better with every sip." He catches Harper's eye at the coffee bar and gives her a thumbs up, and she gives him two back.

"Now, the third step is gauging feedback," Barry says. "Finally, there's the last step. When you get feedback, commit to making changes and actually following through. Nothing erodes trust faster than giving feedback to someone—especially a leader—and seeing no change."

"Sure," Tim says. "People don't like being ignored."

"Right," Barry says. "When people see their feedback leads to positive changes, it strengthens trust. Also, fostering a culture where feedback flows *both* ways is key. Encourage your team to give you feedback regularly and show them you're willing to act on it. This creates a psychologically safe environment where everyone feels valued, and that leads to better outcomes for the whole team."

Tim sits back, looking at his notes.

Radical Candor Feedback Model
1. Get feedback (by asking for it).
2. Give feedback: Situation-Behavior-Impact (SBI) Model.
3. Act on feedback.

"This is great, Barry," he says after a moment. "I can see how this could really turn my team dynamics around. My team might be kind of shocked at first, honestly."

Barry nods. "They'll be shocked in a good way," he says. "Everyone wants to work in an environment where they feel safe to speak up, give and receive feedback, and grow together. That's how you build a strong, cohesive, and effective team."

"How can I start implementing this?" Tim asks, saving his document and sitting back with his cup. "It's going to be a huge change."

"I do have some homework to help you with that," Barry says, picking up his phone. "I'll send over the leadership worksheet right now. You've done a great job identifying your purpose, but that will only go as far as your relationships, your emotional intelligence, and your support for others."

"Yeah," Tim says. "I can kinda see it now. How it's all connected and how important it is to trust others and multiply your reach. I thought identifying a purpose was such a big deal, but it was just the beginning."

"Absolutely," Barry affirms, neatly folding his napkin and muffin wrapper. "You started with your purpose, and now you get to let your team in on that. You're one person, but with other people, you can really make a difference. I hope that worksheet will help you find the right approach for your team."

"I'll make sure to get started on that book too," Tim says, then runs a hand through his hair. "Oh, wow. This is going to be really hard."

Barry grins broadly. "You can do it! Your people will be stronger for it. When you focus on your people and act as a multiplier instead of a diminisher, you're not just building a business—you're building a community. And that's what truly makes the difference."

"Okay," Tim says. "I'll do my best. I'll have that worksheet filled out for next week."

Barry stands up, slapping a twenty-dollar bill onto the table. "Really ponder this one. Next week, we'll review it together and look at a whole new angle on the 'people' side."

Chapter 4 Summary

The Three P's: People—Leadership

What Makes a Great Vision
- Rooted in the organization's values and purpose.
- Ambitious and inspiring goals that motivate your team.
- Clearly articulated.
- Aligned with action and properly executed.

Radical Candor Feedback Model

	→ **Challenging Directly** →	
↑ **Caring Personally**	**Ruinous empathy** Caring a lot but not challenging people enough	**Radical candor** Caring personally while challenging directly
	Manipulative insincerity Neither caring nor challenging	**Obnoxious aggression** Challenging directly without caring enough[13]

---
13 Wiseman and McKeown, *Multipliers*.

- Get feedback (by asking for it).
- Give feedback using the Situation-Behavior-Impact (SBI) Model.
- Act on feedback.

Workplace Culture and Growth
- Focus on long-term business sustainability through strong leadership.
- Build a team-centered environment that encourages collaboration and trust.

Leadership and Vision Worksheet

The first job of a leader—at work or at home—is to inspire trust. It's to bring out the best in people by entrusting them with meaningful stewardships, and to create an environment in which high-trust interaction inspires creativity and possibility.
—**Stephen Covey**[14]

Leadership/Vision

Restate your personal vision here.

To better everyone around me by serving them.

With this in mind and in the context of what is possible for revenue generation, what is your vision for your company?

To improve lives through excellence and service. If we deliver on this, we will be successful.

---

14 Stephen M.R. Covey, *Trust and Inspire: How Truly Great Leaders Unleash Greatness in Others* (Simon & Schuster, 2022).

Diminish/Multiply

> *It is time we recognize that it is not the genius who is at the top of the intelligence hierarchy but rather the genius maker.*
> —Liz Wiseman[15]

Do I meet dissent and errors with negativity?
Yes. I need to work on this.

Does my team hide their errors?
Yes. I'm learning this is the case.

Do I always insist on my own way?
No. I'm too exhausted to do that.

Do I have to step in and manage because my team can't manage themselves?
Often

Am I afraid to fail?
Yes

When I provide feedback, is my focus on criticism instead of development?
Yes. I realize I need to get much better at this.

---

15 Elizabeth Allen Wiseman, "Liz Wiseman on the Power of Not Knowing," *Y Magazine* (Fall 2016), https://magazine.byu.edu/article/power-not-knowing.

Am I the only one who takes ownership? Do I skirt blame sometimes?

This seems to be the case.

If you answered yes to any of these questions, it's time to make a change.

Culture and Feedback

> *Radical candor is humble, it's helpful, it's immediate, it's specific, and it doesn't personalize.*
> —**Kim Scott**[16]

On a scale of 1–4 (4 being the best), rate yourself on:
- Challenging directly: *4*
- Caring personally: *2*

Based on your answer, determine where you fall. Use (challenging directly, caring personally) to review your score:
- Manipulative insincerity: (1,1), (1,2), (2,1), (2,2)
- Ruinous empathy: (1,3), (1,4), (2,3), (2,4)
- Obnoxious aggression: (3,1), (4,1), (3,2), (4,2)
- Radical candor: (3,3), (3,4), (4,3), (4,4)

(4, 2) Obnoxious aggression. Great.

---
16 Scott, *Radical Candor*.

If you really want to take this seriously, have your team and family rate you anonymously.

I think I was brutally honest with myself here!

Do you need work in the following feedback areas?

Getting feedback:

I don't go out of my way to seek feedback. I'm responsible for setting that tone for the organization.

Giving feedback:

I'm not afraid to provide feedback, but I can do so with more empathy. I also realize I need to listen more and seek to understand before providing my own feedback.

Acting on feedback:

My team is afraid to give feedback, so I can't really act on it. I need to encourage this and praise it to get more of it. This will build trust.

Learn more about leadership and vision and download a blank, printable version of this worksheet at ScalableBusinessFramework.com.

Chapter 5

Team

Today, Tim takes Barry's video call from his office at Fast-Track. He desperately misses his quadruple-shot macchiato, making do with a sad cup of drip coffee instead. Outside, the watery January sun tries to pierce a blanket of clouds.

At least I have a muffin, he thinks, unpacking his bag from Robin. She made another batch of the bran and cran muffins after he told her how well they'd gone over at the last meeting.

The clock strikes 1:00 p.m., Tim clicks the link, and Barry's cheerful face appears on the screen.

"Good afternoon, Tim," Barry says.

"Hi, Barry. How are you? Or, should I ask, *where* are you? Is that the ocean behind you?"

"Yes! South Carolina," Barry replies cheerfully. He seems to be sitting on a deck overlooking a sparkling stretch of ocean, the sun bright overhead. "That marathon I told you about was yesterday. We got a rental for the rest of the week."

"Oh," Tim says, looking morosely out at the cloudy winter day. "How did it go?"

"Really, really well," Barry says. "My wife, my kids, and I all ran it. A little sore today, but it could be worse."

"Congratulations," Tim says. "One of these days, I'll find time to start working out again, I swear."

"One step at a time," Barry says. "Now, I know we went over a lot of information at our last meeting. How did your homework go?"

"It was ... enlightening," Tim says. "I scanned my worksheet before our meeting this time since we're doing this virtually. It's in your inbox, grease stains and all."

"Don't worry about that," Barry says, and Tim hears the clicking of keys as he pulls out his own crumpled paper copy of the worksheet. "But before we get into the worksheet, I believe there were a few follow-up items you had to take care of based on the purpose worksheet."

"Yes!" Tim says, remembering. "We talked about letting people know what was going on. I didn't really do it in a formal sense—as in, I didn't call a company or family meeting to tell everyone about my change in perspective—but I have started talking about it and making changes in a really transparent way, which basically accomplishes the same thing."

"And how is everyone reacting?" Barry asks.

"Well, Robin is ecstatic, as you know from the muffins," Tim says with a grin. "She's been begging me to make a change for years, but I just felt so stuck. As for my team, they seem a little cautious, but mostly optimistic."

"Good, good," Barry says, lifting a blue mug into Tim's view. "And how about the Radical Candor feedback model? Did you have time to start implementing that?"

"Again, sort of informally," Tim says. "During meetings, I started asking for feedback and actually writing things down. And when I gave feedback, I tried to use the SBI Model so I was giving actionable steps rather than just snapping at people to do better." Tim laughs. "Go figure—it seems to be more effective. I think one reason I've felt like I had to pull all this weight on my own for so long is because I wasn't actually asking my team to improve. I just expected them to read my mind."

"Wait, they can't read your mind?" Barry asks, giving the camera a mock-startled look.

"I know," Tim says. "I had to give them feedback to work on that."

The two men share a chuckle, and Tim leans back in his chair, glancing at his notes. "This week's worksheet gave me a lot to think about. It wasn't pretty."

Barry leans forward slightly, the ocean glinting in the background as he looks at his computer screen. "That's okay. It sounds like you did a good job starting to implement what we discussed last week, so let's move on to the leadership worksheet now. Start with your personal vision. What did you come up with?"

Tim clears his throat. "I came up with: 'To better everyone around me by serving them.' That's been my guiding principle, and it's what I want to stay focused on."

Barry smiles. "I like that. It's in line with your purpose as well. How does that translate into your vision for FastTrack?"

"I landed on this: 'To improve lives through excellence and service.' If we deliver on that, success will follow, I think. Like you said, making a positive impact leads to financial success in the end."

"A clear and compelling vision," Barry says. "Now, let's dig into the questions about your leadership style. The diminish/multiply section—what stood out to you there?"

Tim hesitates. "That was a real wake-up call. I suspect I'm both a diminisher and an obnoxious aggressor."

"That's okay," Barry says. "It takes a lot to be honest with yourself and admit that. What's your plan to shift that dynamic?"

Tim flips to another page in his notes. "First, I need to set the tone by being open about my own mistakes and creating an environment where it feels *safe* to give feedback and contribute. I also need to move away from just criticizing and focus on development—giving feedback that helps my team grow instead of just barking at them to do better. I already started with that this week, as you know."

Sighing, Tim props his elbow on the desk and rests his chin in his hand. "I think I've been so focused on results that I've neglected relationships with both my team and my family," he admits. "If I want radical candor, I need to show everyone that I care. That means listening more, being present, and encouraging feedback. I've been thinking about holding an anonymous feedback session. I know it'll be brutal, but I've got to rip off the Band-Aid, you know?"

Barry wrinkles his brow. "I have to ask...why anonymous?"

"I just want to make sure they feel safe sharing their thoughts," Tim says.

"I completely understand. May I make a suggestion?"

"Of course."

"What about having a one-on-one feedback session with each team member?" Barry says. "I have found that anonymous feedback is antithetical to building a good culture. On the other hand, you can earn trust by letting each person know that you're actively trying to change and want their help to make yourself and the company better."

"Ah," Tim says, typing this into his notes. "I can see how that would be better. Then I need to show them that I take their input seriously by acting on it."

"That sounds like a great idea. Anything else?"

"Well, I realize I need to gauge feedback better once I get it," Tim says. "I normally tend to jump in with my opinion too quickly. I need to listen more and seek to understand my team's perspective before responding."

Barry leans back, looking thoughtful. "The highest overall predictor of success for a leader is self-awareness, and these are significant steps toward that. If you can build trust and foster open communication, I think it will transform your leadership and your team's performance. How do you feel about this plan?"

Tim smiles faintly. "I feel hopeful, actually. For the first time, I see a clear path forward."

"I can't wait to hear about how this changes your company culture," Barry says with a huge smile. "We'll be sure to follow up on it. In the meantime, I want to introduce you to the topic of the day, which is deeply related to the work you're doing right now."

Barry's voice crackles slightly over the connection as a breeze ruffles his hair. "Today, we'll be talking about the team aspect of the second P—people, which we started on last week. This will define the types of people you attract and retain."

As Tim creates a new heading in his notes, Barry continues talking. "Having a clear team directive like you've identified over the past week will help you build a company like the one you've envisioned, where people are fulfilled by the work they do and don't have a J-O-B. That's what ensures your people enjoy their work."

"Okay," Tim says slowly. "That does sound nice. I have a question, though."

"Sure," Barry says.

"Your employees are there to run your business, not just to hang out and enjoy themselves, right?" Tim says, twisting his empty muffin wrapper into a thin line. "How does that actually play out in day-to-day operations?"

Barry chuckles. "A common concern," he says. "Actually, the first part is something you've already started to implement: integration of your work and your life. For me, flexibility is key to maintaining an integrated life. In fact, at Charis Strategies, flexibility is our people principle, much like impact is our purpose principle."

"Hey, I don't think you told me impact is your first P," Tim says, eyes widening. "That's a good one."

"Thanks," Barry says. "What do you think of flexibility?"

"I'm not so sure about that one," says Tim.

"Flexibility," affirms Barry with a little laugh. "First of all, flexibility is something I personally value and enjoy. For example, I've worked from Indiana, Colorado, Minnesota, Wisconsin, even abroad—pretty much wherever I happen to be. Today, that's Charleston. That freedom allows me to travel, meet new people, and experience different places without skipping a beat in my work."

"Meanwhile, I practically lived in my office up until recently," Tim says, gazing at the seascape behind Barry enviously. "I've slept here more times than I can count, actually. I don't even remember the last time I went on vacation."

Barry nods, leaning back in his Adirondack chair. Tim notices he's wearing a Hawaiian shirt with flamingos on it.

"I hear you," Barry says. "Not being tied to a desk for nine or ten hours a day and being able to actively participate in my family's life has been the absolute best change for me."

"Yeah," Tim says. "That makes sense."

"I want to emphasize that at Charis Strategies, flexibility is not just for leaders," Barry says. "For example, everyone works from home."

"*Everyone?*" Tim is aghast.

"Everyone," Barry affirms, holding his hands apart for emphasis. "We don't even have an office. We've been doing this since I started the company ten years ago."

"That explains why you're at La Chance so much," Tim says.

"Yes, and in places like this," Barry says with a smile, glancing around at his sun-drenched scenery.

"Okay, well, as great as that sounds, it's not an option for me," Tim says. "An HVAC business needs on-site staff."

"That's true," Barry says. "Flexibility is the people concept that works for Charis Strategies specifically. Since your business is very different, it might not work for you. But some of the underlying principles may be the same. Every business needs to figure out what kind of environment aligns with their goals and values."

"Got it," Tim says, mollified.

"Say, is that a bran and cran muffin you're eating?"

"Sure is," Tim says, smiling as he lifts his snack.

"Could you send one over here for me?" Barry says. "Seriously, though. I need the recipe for those."

"I can get it for you," Tim says, smiling. "But I'm sure Robin would be happy to send you a steady supply. She's so happy with the changes she's seeing in me already, as am I. Christa even seems slightly less disgruntled when I give her baths now. Slightly."

"Love to hear it," Barry says merrily. "To get back on track here, you'll have to figure out your people principle on your own. That being said, I do want to present the example of Beacon, since they offer on-site services like you do."

"Yes, I'd love to hear that," Tim says.

"All the administrative staff at Beacon who don't need to be on-site work from home," Barry says. "They offer their service teams flexible schedules and reasonable hours where possible."

"Hmm," Tim says. "Doesn't that affect productivity and the bottom line?"

"It does. It *improves* productivity and the bottom line."

Tim raises an eyebrow involuntarily. Barry leans toward the screen, his tanned face blocking out some of the seascape.

"I believe work is a good thing, especially when you're doing what you love," Barry says. "I also believe life is best when it's fully integrated. You shouldn't have to choose between raising your kids and doing meaningful work. We can't expect our team to pour into each other and our customers from an empty cup. That's why we built an environment where people can have fully integrated lives."

Tim sits back, thinking about the recent changes he's made to his own life. Doesn't he want the same for his employees? Is that even possible?

"This system lets everyone who doesn't have to be on-site be with their families, skip the commute, and live wherever they want," Barry says. "At the same time, our employees manage their own schedules so they can balance life and work. This has the end result of fostering a committed team that truly loves what they do and works hard to make sure the business succeeds."

Tim leans his head on his hand and listens. Barry stretches back, and the sea sparkles behind him.

"Our people can watch their kids grow up, go on dates, and enjoy whatever season of life they're in," Barry is saying, his eyes unfocused. "We don't micromanage, and we give them the flexibility to live their lives while loving the work they do. It gives them a sense of autonomy. They can plan their day the way that works best for them."

Tim heaves a sigh and types some notes. "Okay, okay," he says. "I get it, and I can see why putting people first is important. But I still don't really see how that doesn't negatively affect productivity. If you afford your employees so much trust and respect that they can just run off to the grocery store or whatever whenever they want, won't that prevent them from working?"

"Our systems definitely require accountability," Barry says, holding his coffee mug lazily by the handle. "At Charis Strategies, our team manages their own schedules, stays available to each other, and makes sure they don't overwork themselves. This is what we call the flexibility principle—it's about creating a balanced environment where people thrive both personally and professionally. The compensation model depends on each person's performance to the standards for their role. Frequent one-on-one meetings keep everything aligned. Even if you're not going for flexibility like we are, that balance and underlying culture are key."

"It sounds like you'd need a specific kind of employee for that," Tim says, thinking out loud. "There are bad actors out there who might not take accountability seriously."

"True," Barry says. "We are pretty careful during our hiring processes at Charis Strategies, and I encourage my business consulting clients—including you, Tim—to do the same. We look for team members based on what Patrick Lencioni calls 'humble, hungry, and smart' in his book *The Ideal Team Player*.[17] I saw his TED Talk several years ago, and it had a big influence on us."

"How do you spell that last name?" Tim asks. "I'd like to look it up."

Barry nods. "Great idea." He spells out the name, then continues. "Anyway, we're looking for those traits before we bring someone on board. When I do bring on new team members, I start by aligning on a cultural level. Charis Strategies is up front about who we are, and we let potential

---

17 Patrick Lencioni, *The Ideal Team Player: How to Recognize and Cultivate the Three Essential Virtues* (Jossey-Bass, 2016).

hires interview us just as much as we interview them. That way, they can be sure they'll be happy and it's a good fit."

Barry looks up as he thinks. Tim absently picks up another muffin, then sets it down. He realizes he isn't really hungry.

"We look at skills and other factors, but we can't have just anyone on the team," Barry muses. "We can teach skills, but we can't teach attitude or hunger. What we *can* do is take people who are driven, have the right mindset, and fit into our culture, and then help them grow—mentoring them and guiding them to where they want to go."

Tim presses his hands to his temples. "So, I have to fire everyone."

"Exactly," Barry says. Tim looks up in surprise, and Barry starts laughing, the sound crackling through the speakers. Tim finds himself laughing along, and his laughter must be carrying, because several of his employees peer curiously at his office from over their cubicles. He waves at them.

"Absolutely not," Barry says, still chuckling. "You'll find that most of your team appreciates any changes you choose to make and takes them in stride. Anyone who can't will likely self-select out. You can make it clear that being aligned culturally and with your purpose is nonnegotiable. At Charis Strategies, we coach people, but if someone can't become an A player, we help them find a better fit elsewhere."

"Okay, got it," Tim says, starting to type. "I don't have to fire everyone, but I do have to start building a team of people who are fully committed to the mission and culture."

"Right," Barry says. "Your team needs to buy into the mission and feel motivated by not just *what* they do but *why* they do it. That commitment is what allows us to serve our clients effectively while also creating a fulfilling work environment for the team."

"So, when I'm hiring, what should I look for?" Tim asks.

"Only you can say," Barry says. "We can talk about that once you've given it some thought. Today's worksheet should help you with that."

Barry looks at something behind the camera, out of Tim's field of vision, and nods. "Tim, I've got to get going here in a minute or two, but I want to leave you with one more thing," he says. "I've been running Charis Strategies for almost ten years now, and as our anniversary approaches, I've been thinking about what's next. I think, for me, there are two things that define success for this business and in general."

"What are they?" Tim asks.

Barry crosses his arms, thinking. "First, when I'm no longer here, the business should do better without me. That would mean I did my job right." He nods as if agreeing with himself. "Second, the people here should have better opportunities without me than they did with me. That's my exit plan—whatever it looks like, as long as we hit those marks, I'm good."

Tim nods. "Focusing on the future. That's a smart approach."

"I hope so," Barry says. "Whether it's selling one day or having the employees take over, it doesn't matter as long as those goals are met. I don't own the whole company anymore—we've got an equity plan in place, and about twenty-seven or twenty-eight employees have ownership now. I'm still the majority shareholder, but the goal is to help them create wealth through this business."

Tim sees how this ties into Barry's focus on people. "You're building more than just a business," he says. "You're creating something lasting for the people who are part of it. That way, they feel truly invested."

Barry nods. "That's the idea. The best part of this whole thing has been watching the team do things better than I ever could. I'm focused on giving them more opportunities and staying out of their way. I'm good at getting things to this point, but I may not be the right person to take it further, and I don't want to slow it down."

Tim leans back, considering Barry's perspective. "I can't say I've ever thought about any of that for FastTrack. I'm too busy trying not to burn everything down to think about what it'll look like in a decade or two."

"I understand," Barry says. "But you're already making strides in the right direction. Leadership is about creating an environment where everyone can thrive, feel valued, and know their contributions matter. You're already recognizing some issues with your leadership style and making changes, and after today, you should have a better perspective on the team you're leading. That's how you build a business that doesn't just succeed but leaves a lasting impact on everyone involved, and I really think that starts from a place of esteem and respect for each person who works for you."

"Hmm," Tim says, mulling this over.

"I recently watched a documentary on Pat Dye, and he said something that resonated with me: 'I'm not smart enough to tell you how much I care about you.'[18] That's exactly how I feel about my team. These folks are a blessing to me. Over my career, I've learned that focusing on who, not what, is crucial."

Tim leans back, absently tossing his muffin wrapper into the trash. It's clear that Barry genuinely cares about his team. This is a new notion for Tim. Does he care about his team? Maybe he should care more.

"This is going to be a massive mindset shift," he says.

"But it'll be so worth it," Barry says. "Creating a workplace where people are motivated and aligned with the company's values is fundamental to success. Approaching your team with intention and integrity changes everything for the better, and I think you'll find the right approach for your business too. Now, I've got to go, but the new worksheet is in your inbox. See you next week?"

---

18 Slats Slaton, dir., *Mighty: The Life and Legacy of Pat Dye*. Alabama Public Television, aired September 25, 2023, https://aptv.org/mighty.

"Next week, with much better coffee," Tim says, and Barry waves. The sun-drenched window closes, and Tim is left staring out into the gray sky beyond his office. A tentative tap at his door snaps him back to reality.

"Mr. Hodges?" Gina says, poking her head in.

"You know what?" Tim waves her in. "You should just call me Tim. How are you, Gina?"

Gina looks so shocked that Tim is tempted to laugh. *Yikes*, he thinks. *I have got to do better.*

Chapter 5 Summary

The Three P's: People—Team

Team Dynamics and Company Culture
- Define a people principle that aligns with company needs and values.
- Challenge traditional on-site work models where appropriate.

Hiring and Talent Strategy
- Prioritize attitude over skills.
- Hire people with the right mindset and cultural fit.
- Train for skills and provide existing talent with feedback and coaching as needed.

Long-Term Vision and Organizational Growth
- Structure the company to thrive beyond the founder's involvement.
- Create opportunities for employees to grow and advance.
- Shift focus from just business success to people development.

Team Worksheet

If you hire people just because they can do a job, they'll work for your money. But if you hire people who believe what you believe, they'll work for you with blood, sweat, and tears.
—Simon Sinek[19]

Standards

How do you define success for your people?

We want our team to be HEROES.

- Honest. Trustworthy. We are open about failure because that's the pathway to improvement. The team has to be honest about how they feel. They are bold enough to challenge each other directly for improvement.

---

19 Simon Sinek, *Start with Why: How Great Leaders Inspire Everyone to Take Action* (Penguin Group, 2009).

- Enthusiastic. They're aligned with our values, and that gives them energy. They carry this energy and positivity in every circumstance, and they don't let anything overcome it or overwhelm them. Why should they? Our team has their back.

- Reflective. They look inward and hold themselves accountable first to their values and our team's values. That means they look to control what they can control and, like Stephen Covey teaches, seek to understand before being understood.

- Open to learn. They are open to feedback and eager to improve. If they are bold enough to challenge directly, they need to be bold enough to accept feedback and learn. Feedback is a gift that sharpens our team and pushes us forward.

- Empathetic. They care about others and put themselves in the other's shoes. They try to see things from the other person's perspective. They reflect on how others might feel and use empathy to navigate difficult situations.

- Solution-oriented. They are problem solvers. They take ownership of every situation and responsibility for the results. They focus on the correct inputs to get the right outputs. They don't complain about the problem—instead, they seek to find a solution.

How do you define excellence in your organization? What are your standards?

Right now, there isn't clarity. I just know when something isn't done well, and I correct it. We've grown large enough where I can't continue to do that. There's no consistency. I need to work with my team to determine what these standards are based on our values.

General

What values do you want your team to embody?

- Servant leadership. We help others reach their full potential by serving and helping them.

- Hustle. We aren't satisfied with the average level of service for our clients. We strive to take it to the next level.

- Detailed. We don't leave a stone unturned or a box unchecked.

When have you seen your team the most unified? What were the circumstances? What values do you find there?

When we're working together to take care of a customer. None of us know all the answers, but we always rally together to take care of the customer and propose the right solutions. I love the team-based atmosphere that we have. There are no lone wolves.

What moment or accomplishment are you most proud of with your current team? What values drove that success?

One story comes to mind. A few years back, there was a freak cold snap, and a Friday evening ice storm caused all kinds of issues for people. We got a lot of emergency calls that day, including one from an elderly single woman whose heat just went out. Our team rallied together to go to her house because we knew it would be a rough night/weekend for her if we couldn't get her heat working again.

Long story short, we came together to get it fixed. She had tears in her eyes as we left. I felt like I'd just made my own grandmother proud. The team was walking on clouds after that, knowing the difference we made in the life of that one person. It was an incredible experience to see how everyone came together to fulfill our mission and purpose.

Are they passionate about what they are doing?

> Yes, our team is passionate and motivated to help our customers. We need to do a better job of defining our roles and responsibilities while highlighting our core values. We have a lot of room for improvement in this area.

Company Culture

If you want clients to trust you, your team needs to trust itself. How do you foster a culture of trust and shared values within your organization?

> We should start by reminding ourselves of the values at every meeting. We have to hold ourselves accountable and really live by these. If someone doesn't, they need to be coached or let go. If we can accomplish this, we'll be on our way to establishing the culture.

Does your team handle conflict in a positive and healthy way? Does it avoid conflict?

> We could do better at this. Sometimes I'm not sure people are pushing back against me or are 100 percent honest. I believe there is some conflict avoidance within the team.

Does your team hold each other accountable?

> No, we haven't set them up with a standard to do this.

Does your team care for each other?
I think most do, but there may be a few who don't.

Does your team prioritize group success over individual achievements?
I believe most do, yes.

Recruitment

What skills and talents are required to work at your company?

- *Hard work is nonnegotiable.*

- *You must be hungry to grow and learn.*

- *You must be empathetic to our customers and your teammates.*

- *You have to know your trade and be an expert on the technical side of the business (for those to whom this applies).*

- *We can teach you additional skills, but striving for excellence is a requirement.*

What type of people will align with your values and be attracted to your purpose?

People who work hard, love to learn, enjoy solving a variety of problems, are great team players, and love making customers happy.

What type of people are not a good fit for your company?

People who want a J-O-B. People that tend to be selfish and aren't focused on helping others. People who don't have the capability to do the technical aspects of the job. People who don't like solving a variety of problems. People who lack empathy.

How will you recruit people to your organization to ensure they're a good fit?

I need to create a recruitment process that verifies their personality, motivations, and values to ensure they align. We also need some technical validation of their skills.

Assessing the Current Team

Is anyone a drain on the culture or a source of negativity? Can they change?

Yes, we definitely have some people who are really talented and very good at solving technical problems but are not good with customers. They may solve the problem, but the customers never feel good about the experience. I can't let them go right now as we don't have enough people to handle all the jobs we have, but something's gotta give.

Do your other employees' values align with your values and what you want for the company?
Yes, for the most part. But I'm not sure we let them know or celebrate them enough. We have a lot of people doing great things, but I'm always dealing with the issues and poor performers. Our best people probably feel underappreciated. We could find a way to highlight the good things they do in front of the rest of the team: maybe send a notification out to the team and also track everything in a system that lets us report on them later and remember our wins.

Do their values and skills also align with the role they are in?
We definitely have a few people who may excel in other roles, but we're not quite big enough for them to move into those roles. This motivates me to grow, but I don't know how to do that yet.

How will you coach people out of your organization who don't fit?
If we are consistent with one-on-one meetings and coaching, we should be able to catch when someone isn't aligned with our values. We need to be transparent with them and help them see it's not going to work out. I would rather free them up for an

opportunity that's a better fit than have them try to fit where it won't work.

How will you develop and serve the people in your organization so they reach their potential?

We will work with them to understand their goals and also relay our goals for them. We'll develop a plan and coach them toward those goals.

How will you ensure you don't avoid difficult conversations with your team?

We need to set up consistent meeting opportunities between team leaders and team members. Some of the principles from Radical Candor by Kim Scott might help (I started listening to it). I believe we need to challenge directly and care personally at every level of the organization. I need to be open about my effort to do this and lead the charge.

How will you create an environment where people want to stay and not leave?

When people leave, it's because they don't want the level of commitment that's required. I think to truly serve our customers like our values state, we need to work hard for them. I need to create a culture where people are brought into those values without feeling burned out or like they're sacrificing something important elsewhere. The "serve" value should give them energy. This means I need to be very consistent in messaging and frequently check in to ensure the team is doing well, isn't burned out, and is all-in on the mission.

Learn more about building a great team and download a blank, printable version of this worksheet at ScalableBusinessFramework.com.

Chapter 6

Clients, Mentorships, and Business Partners

The large window behind Barry frames a gray February sky, but inside the coffee shop, there's a lot of extra color today. Strings of heart-shaped lights hang across the ceiling, and the counter is lined with pink and red Valentine's Day treats.

Tim walks up to Barry's table just as a man in a thick sweater and jeans leaves. The man gives Tim a friendly wave on his way out.

"Hi, Tim," Barry says, gesturing to the newly vacated seat. Tim takes it, setting down his coffee cup. The smell of freshly baked pastries mixes with the hum of soft conversation around them.

Tim glances at his mentor, who is taking a long sip from his yellow cup, wearing his typical activewear, and looking completely at ease.

"Back to our spot," Barry says, nodding with a smile.

"Yeah, it's good to be here again instead of on a video call," Tim replies, setting a small bag on the table. "Picked up something from the counter."

Barry raises an eyebrow, amused. "No muffins today?"

Tim grins as he places a couple of heart-shaped cookies on the table between them. "Well, it's February. Seemed fitting."

Barry laughs and reaches for one of the cookies. "You're getting into the spirit, huh?"

Tim shrugs. "Why not? I've been feeling a little more love lately. I even dragged my two oldest out into the backyard over the weekend on that sunny day, and we got to work on their batting and throwing. Practice starts in a few weeks, and they're a little rusty."

"That's great!" Barry says. "How'd they do?"

"I'm more worried about how I did," Tim says, laughing. "Both kids have great throwing arms on them, but I'm so out of shape, it's a little alarming. I was losing my breath just running around the yard. I think it might be time for me to start sneaking a few workouts in here and there."

"I certainly feel better when I'm active," Barry says.

"When aren't you active?" Tim says, laughing.

"Hey, I went through a phase just like you're going through now," Barry says. "But I got back on the treadmill, so to speak, and here we are. Now, let's get back into it. Tell me about your homework."

"Actually, before we talk about the team worksheet, can I tell you a little about those one-on-one feedback sessions?" Tim asks. "I started them this past week."

"Yes, please do!" Barry says, picking up his pink mug.

"I set up those sessions to start changing the culture and to encourage people to give me real feedback," Tim explains. "It was hard, but I had to be thorough."

"What did you do in these meetings?" Barry asks.

"Well, first, I had to let them know I was serious about improving myself and the business and that I need their help," Tim says. "Then I asked them questions like, 'What can I do to improve? What can I stop doing?' I had to really listen, thank them, and present them with a plan to address the feedback. I also told them to hold me accountable to fix it."

"That's great, Tim," Barry says. "That does sound hard, and I'm impressed that you were so thorough. So, did it pay off? What did you learn?"

"Well, one thing I learned is that I struggle with letting my team take ownership," Tim says, absently ripping up a napkin. "I'm very caught up in the details and don't let my team develop solutions on their own. I just march in like Napoleon and tell them what to do. My team feels that I also don't listen well, and I've learned I need to listen to understand and not just think of my next point."

"Ah," Barry says. "I have to say, a lot of that reflects issues you identified on your own in that leadership worksheet."

"Sure does," Tim says grumpily. "It hurts to stare your own faults in the face like this, but at least I have a pretty concrete picture of what I need to do: shut up and listen."

Amused, Barry looks at the pile of shredded napkins now sitting atop their table as Tim pulls out his worksheet. "You're clearly a good listener in our sessions. I have no doubt listening to your team will come easily to you once you make this mental shift."

Tim puts the worksheet on the table. This time, he carefully put it into a stiff folder and kept it free of stains. Barry smiles as he looks over Tim's answers.

"Your answer to defining success for your people is really intriguing," he says. "Can you tell me about that?"

Tim sits up straighter. "I want my people to be HEROES," he says. "Honest, enthusiastic, reflective, open to learning, empathetic, and solution-oriented."

Barry claps his hands. "That's incredible, Tim. I love the acrostic. Very catchy."

"Thanks," Tim says. "I was pretty proud of that one."

"Do you feel your team is currently made up of HEROES?"

"Well, yes, sometimes," Tim says. "I realized the team is at its best when we rally around a shared mission. Like that time we had a bad storm and a bunch of people lost heat. The whole team came together, drove through dangerous conditions, and got people's heat running. It was hard work, but it was also incredibly rewarding."

Barry smiles. "That's a beautiful story. It lines up nicely with your people principle of service."

"Oh, for sure," Tim says. "But those moments are few and far between."

"What do you think you need to change?" Barry asks, lifting his mug. "Let's start talking about some action steps you can take."

"Well, I want our entire people methodology, starting with the HEROES model, to be clear and at the front of everyone's mind," Tim says.

"How could you accomplish that?" asks Barry.

"Maybe we could put it on our office wall and in an internal website section that everyone has access to so we can provide lots of details. I'm going to repeat it often in meetings as well," Tim says, taking out a pen and scribbling some notes in the margin of his worksheet.

"Very good ideas," Barry says. "My team could all recite our values and Three P's directives by heart. Speaking of which, did you think at all about what your ideal employee is like?"

"Yeah," Tim says. "I realized they need to be hard workers, eager to learn, problem solvers, and empathetic teammates. We have plenty of people like that now, but the truth is, I'm not always setting them up for success. And we definitely need a better recruitment process to ensure new hires fit our culture."

Barry nods sympathetically, his eyes on the worksheet. "Can you tell me about this?" he asks, pointing at the "Assessing the Current Team" section.

"Well," Tim says, "I've got some really talented folks who are great at solving technical problems, but they have zero social skills," Tim says with a little smile. "They fix things, but they just aren't... tactful, you know? They don't leave the customer feeling good about the experience."

"Understandable," Barry says. "What's your plan there?"

"I'm sure I could give those employees some training or put them in roles that don't require interfacing with customers," Tim says. "I also have to set up consistent meetings to catch issues early and lead by example."

Barry taps his fingers on his mug. "Let's talk about how you might make a bit of a culture shift to that effect. In this worksheet, you answered a lot of questions about your team as a whole, such as whether their skills and values align with their current role and whether they are passionate about what they do. What if you made a list of everyone on your team and answered these questions for them individually? What kinds of follow-up actions could you take?"

Tim scribbles a note in the margin, then looks up. "I don't know why I didn't think of that," he says. "If they're passionate, but their skills don't align, I need to work on hiring more people so I have the flexibility to move current employees to new roles. If their skills align, but they aren't passionate, we need to coach them on the 'why' more. And if they don't have skill and value alignment and they aren't passionate, then we may need to get them off the bus."

"Right," Barry says. "It might lead to some hard conversations and changes, but everyone will be better off in the long run. Now, one more thing. How's the team handling conflict and accountability right now?"

Tim looks down at the worksheet. "Not great. I've noticed some conflict avoidance, and people probably don't push back on me enough. We haven't established a strong culture of accountability even though most of the team genuinely cares about each other and the mission."

"Well, identifying these issues will likely go a long way toward fixing them," Barry says. "It sounds like right now, your entire process around people is reactionary, which probably isn't helping. What do you think you can do to create a proactive approach that promotes your values?"

"Uh," Tim says, "I'm honestly not sure. Could you put me on the right track?"

"Of course," Barry says. "Think about feedback and meetings. How often do your employees meet with their managers for feedback and coaching?"

"Hmm," Tim says. "Never?"

Barry chuckles. "How often do you think they should be doing this?"

Tim looks up at the ceiling, thinking. "What about once a month?" he suggests.

"That's exactly what I recommend," Barry says. "A regular monthly cadence of one-on-one meetings between each employee and their manager fosters a proactive environment to provide feedback and coach a team to success. It also helps train managers to give direct feedback while maintaining a high level of empathy for each team member. This culture will produce real-time feedback in regular meetings; employees shouldn't hold their feedback for one-on-ones. If you implement it well, you'll never be surprised by feedback during a one-on-one. And don't forget—consistency is key. You have to stick to a regular schedule and prioritize those one-on-one meetings. It's easy to fall back into bad habits if you don't stay consistent."

Tim scrawls a note for himself on his worksheet. "I really like that idea," he says. "Thanks."

"Sure thing," Barry says. "You've done a lot of great work here, and I think if you make these changes, you'll see a huge difference."

"I think so too." Tim smiles as he puts his worksheet away. The coffee shop is absolutely stuffed with people; there seems to be some kind of retirees' get-together that has taken up the entire back corner of the shop.

"Now, let's forge ahead," Barry says, scooting forward as a man with a walker makes his way past, clutching a paperback novel. "Last time, we talked a lot about our people within the company. Today will be the last day we discuss people. Let's start with another crucial group: the people *outside* the company."

Tim leans forward. "You mean clients?"

"Clients," Barry agrees. "One of my core beliefs is that the happiness of my clients is nonnegotiable. If the clients aren't happy, nothing else matters."

"The customer is always right,"Tim quips, taking a bite of his sugar cookie.

"No, actually, I have to disagree," Barry says. "It goes much deeper than that. I think relationships with clients should be just as people-centric as relationships within our teams. You want to truly understand and empathize with clients instead of just completing the job. Prioritizing relationships makes you more profitable, not less. And much like building a team, you have to make sure you find the right clients. Not all clients are good clients."

"People who need HVAC?" Tim says mildly. Barry chuckles.

"Well, let me use Charis Strategies as an example again, keeping in mind that our markets are quite different. Focusing on the right clients is essential. To maintain a healthy business that supports both our team and our clients, we have to be selective. Our clients expect results, hold us accountable, and stay motivated to improve their lives and businesses. Complacency isn't an option on either side."

Tim sits back for a moment, seizing his mug. "So, you're not just taking on any client who comes your way?"

"Definitely not," Barry affirms. "We expect our clients to value our work, pay us well, and want us to succeed as true partners. We all need to be in it for the long haul.

We've developed an offering that targets a specific market. This approach helps us say yes to the right clients—the ones with the right mentality. And it also means we can say no to those who aren't ready to make that investment."

Tim seems to ponder this. "That makes me feel special, I guess."

Barry laughs. "I could see that you were ready to make a change. You're in it to win it. You and our other clients value what we offer because our service stands out and meets our customers' needs. It's called product-market fit, and these characteristics are part of our ideal customer profile."

Tim nods. "Yeah, that makes a lot of sense. What I was doing was killing me, and I'm sure plenty of other people have the same issue. So, you're not afraid to turn clients away? I can't imagine doing that."

Barry nods. "Not everyone is willing to do what it takes, and that's okay. We attract like-minded individuals who are passionate about their work. That way, we're not just providing a service—we're building a partnership where both sides are committed to success."

Tim nods. "So, part of your strategy is qualifying the right *kind* of clients who are ready to invest in what you offer."

Barry smiles. "Yes, and it starts with how we recruit and develop both our team and our clients."

"Recruiting clients," Tim snorts. "Now, there's a novel thought."

"Quite a flip from scrounging for them, yes," Barry says. "At Charis Strategies, we have a very intentional client recruitment process. I have several employees whose sole job is to visit referral partner offices and build relationships. That's still where some of my marketing dollars go. We do have a marketing team, but we're marketing not only to our target audience but also to referral partners and candidates—because we're in the people business."

Tim sits back, munching his cookie and listening. This is a very different way of looking at acquiring clients.

"Our marketing team helps us recruit people, both clients and team members, whom we can build up for the long haul," Barry explains. "I call it 'growing people up to stay.' We also market to referral reps with content, stories, case studies, and materials that show how we can help them sell more."

Tim looks up at the Valentine's Day garland above him, thinking. "That's a smart approach for what you're doing. It sounds like you're building a community of partners who are invested in each other's success rather than a typical client base."

Barry smiles as a nearby table bursts into hoarse laughter. "That's the idea," he says over the uproar. "We also market directly to customers by speaking to their specific problems and showing how our company is their guide to overcoming them. We have to look deeper to determine the real problems they deal with beyond the surface need for our service. If we can show prospects that we can solve those deeper issues, which are often emotional ones, we can connect and build trust with them. That creates stronger, more dynamic relationships."

Barry holds his mug in both hands. "To add to that, our primary go-to-market strategy is through our referral network. We track everything in our CRM[20]—and I mean everything—which means we track hundreds of referrals every month. Our conversion rate is around 20 percent. We don't just know who the best referral partners are; we know why we're winning and why we're losing. Our sales team is basically making sure we get the right type of client—someone who aligns with our mission and values our services. Given that, you might assume we're pretty expensive."

Tim raises an eyebrow. "I'm familiar with your rates."

Barry chuckles. "We're not Planet Fitness; we're more like a CrossFit gym. You have to be serious about it, want to get in shape, and be willing to spend money. We're not looking to just collect ten dollars a month from clients who never show up. Our pricing reflects the value and commitment we bring, and we seek clients who are equally committed."

"Okay, I like that analogy," Tim says. "Joining a gym doesn't get you in shape; doing the work does."

"Exactly," Barry says. "You skipped over the qualification part by approaching me directly. I could tell you were desperate and really needed this, so we bypassed all of that."

---

20 CRM (Customer Relationship Management system)

"Yeah, I really was," Tim says. "Thanks for taking me on."

"Happy to do it," Barry says. "But usually we do screen clients. If they don't have real pain and a true desire to get healthy, they won't appreciate it, and they're not ready. We can build the best system in the world, but if they're not going to use it, what's the point?"

"Well, I was definitely in pain," Tim says, laughing. "I can see how that's important."

Barry smiles, leaning down to pick up a large metal water bottle. "We just want to ensure that our clients are fully engaged and committed, which ensures our team is working with people who truly want us to make an impact. It's a win-win." He takes a long drink of water. "But on the sales side, the biggest reason people don't buy from us is because they decide not to buy into a CRM. They're not quite ready to join the CrossFit gym. For various reasons—whether it's the cost or something else—they don't commit. They have to pay for both a CRM platform and our services, and that's by far the number one reason people don't go forward. We haven't gotten to that point, but it's a discussion I was going to broach with you over the next few weeks."

Tim frowns. "I already have a CRM, and it's not doing much for me."

Barry's eyes sparkle. "We've started with more of the theory and philosophy components. We'll get to the CRM and other practical application steps starting next week."

Barry sets his water bottle down next to his chair again. Above him, the heart-shaped streamers flutter briefly as someone opens the door to La Chance.

"Now, I want to discuss another people component," Barry says.

"Okay," Tim says. "You mean like personal relationships?"

"Specifically mentorships," Barry says. "When I think about the people in my life, there's no question that I wouldn't be where I am today without them. My parents, wife, kids . . . of course. But from a business perspective, mentorships can be equally formative."

Barry breaks off another piece of cookie, examining the sparkling, sugary frosting. "I have a friend, Laura, who studied computer science and graduated as a software engineer," he says. "Just like a lot of us back then, she started out writing code. She told me that one of her professors, who also ran a professional services firm, had her working on large-scale enterprise applications for Fortune 1000 companies. Back then, you built everything from scratch—none of the tools we have now."

Tim blows out a breath. "Sounds like a pain."

"It was," Barry says with a laugh. "But Laura loves that kind of thing. She always knew she wanted to be in software, but she wasn't sure whether to join a big company or a small one, or go to grad school. She was accepted to Georgia Tech, but then her professor offered her a job."

"Wow!" Tim says.

"It was really exciting," Barry says. "Laura was one of the first employees at the company, working on some incredible projects. That's where she met two of her mentors, and those mentorships made a huge impact on her career."

Tim nods, listening.

"Laura's mentors gave her a huge amount of responsibility and let her make mistakes without guilt," Barry explains. "She was talking with CIOs at some of the biggest companies in the world when she was only twenty-two! She told me she didn't feel like she belonged in those rooms, but she learned so much. The company grew from fifteen to one hundred fifty employees in just six years."

"Is Laura still working there?" Tim asks.

"No, she actually started her own business," Barry says, taking a nibble of cookie. "But the way they treated her and the opportunities they gave her were foundational. Those early experiences gave her the confidence to start her own business. Laura didn't know she would end up an entrepreneur—she just wanted to write code back then."

Tim nods. "It sounds like they saw something in her before she saw it herself," he says, looking back at Barry.

Barry smiles. "Exactly. Being trusted by people at that level and getting to have those conversations—it was a blessing. When someone believes in you early on, it gives you the confidence to push forward."

Tim nods, thinking of Bertha. "Mentorship can really change the course of your life."

Barry nods. "Absolutely. Mentorship doesn't just teach you skills—it gives you the belief that you can do something great. That's what truly sets you on the path to success. As a leader and mentor, it's tough not to get emotional when things go wrong, but you have to take the high road—even when it's hard. Your business is your baby, but not everyone will love it like you do."

Tim leans in, nodding. "It's tough not to take things personally."

"Exactly," Barry says. "Laura told me that when she decided to leave and move to a product company, her mentors could've been upset—she was a key leader, and she had a lot of responsibilities. But instead, they supported her. They even helped her set up her next venture. That taught her a lot about taking the high road."

Tim, surprised, asks, "And they just let her go?"

Barry nods. "Mm-hmm. They kept supporting her, opened doors, and stayed friends and mentors. They showed her what it means to truly care about people's growth, even if it's not in your own best interest."

Tim smiles, then frowns. "That wouldn't be my first inclination."

Barry nods, picking up his mug. "Looking back, I treat people the way I do now because of how lucky I was with mentors. I know I often caused them extra work, but they never put that on me. When you invest in people like that, you get tremendous blessings. Some of the people who've left Charis Strategies are out there doing amazing things, and I'm proud of that. I still mentor some of them. Those relationships are some of your biggest challenges but also where your greatest blessings come from. And that," Barry says with a smile, "is a great segue into relationships as a whole."

"Like marriage and such? Friendships?"

"Not quite," Barry says, picking up his last cookie shard. "Business relationships. Whether they're with your team, your clients, your partners, your mentors—relationships are the real currency of business. Trust, character, and shared values makes everything else flow more easily. Relationships come first, and business follows naturally."

Tim, thoughtful, says, "That's true, I guess."

Barry smiles. "When you have trust, hard conversations become easier, and solving problems becomes the focus. You don't need a team where everyone agrees—you need trust and shared values. Take one of my clients, Jeff. He was working a regular job when he reconnected with Gale, a business strategist he knew from years ago. They got to talking and realized they both had a vision to start something of their own.

"Jeff told me that Gale asked him to quit his job and take the risk with her to start a new company," Barry explains. "It wasn't an easy decision, but it felt like the right move for both of them."

"So, how'd they do?" Tim asks, thinking of how scary that sounds.

"They started the business out of Gale's house," Barry says. "It wasn't glamorous, but they worked hard, and the experience was incredible for both of them. It taught them a lot about trust, taking risks, and building something from scratch. Today, their company is very profitable."

Tim nods, swirling the last of his coffee around in the bottom of his mug. "Sounds like they've had some amazing people around them."

Barry smiles. "They really have. The partnership between Jeff and Gale was key to their success, and seeing them build that business was a great reminder of how important the right collaboration can be. Teams can be horizontal instead of just vertical, and surrounding yourself with great people makes all the difference."

Tim starts typing again. "I like that idea," he says. "Horizontal, not just vertical."

Barry smiles, then drains his cup. "Exactly. That connects back to leadership as well."

Tim saves his notes on his computer, checks the time, and snaps his computer closed. "Got it. I'll get out of your hair. Do you have a worksheet for me this week?"

"Already in your inbox," Barry says. "Can't wait to see what you come up with."

Chapter 6 Summary

The Three P's: People—Clients, Mentorships, and Business Partners

Client Relationships and Acquisition

Strong Client Partnerships
- Choose clients who value your product or service and vision.
- Focus on long-term relationships over transactional deals.

Client Acquisition
- Leverage referral partners to recruit new clients.
- Create a community of engaged and invested partners.

Mentorship and Business Relationships
- Trust and shared values make up the foundation of strong relationships inside and outside your business.
- Support mentee development to strengthen your team and business.

Clients, Mentorships, and Business Partners Worksheet

I have learned that the best way to lift one's self up is to help someone else.
—Booker T. Washington[21]

Clients

Instead of focusing on the competition, focus on the customer.
—Scott Cook[22]

Who is your ideal client?

> A homeowner who has a problem with their HVAC system and doesn't know what to do or how to fix it. Our best customers are the ones who are stressed out and scared that the repair is going to be very

---

21 Booker T. Washington, *The Story of My Life and Work* (W. H. Ferguson Co., 1900), 277, scanned copy available online from Smithsonian Libraries, https://library.si.edu/digital-library/book/storyofmylifewor00wash.
22 Scott Cook, "PC Magazine Catches Up with the Intuit Founder, Our Newest Lifetime Achievement Award Winner," interview by Michael Miller, *PC Magazine*, November 18, 2003, https://www.pcmag.com/archive/interview-scott-cook-112718.

expensive. We specialize in helping the homeowner get through the situation while offering multiple solutions they can afford. We provide joy and peace during a difficult time for our customers.

How will you find and attract your ideal customers?
Historically, we've managed by word of mouth. But it's becoming tricky to track lead sources and grow our customer base.

How do you ensure your clients align with your values and vision? How can you ensure your team can identify these clients?
For our area of business, I think it will be important to focus on team training for now. We can look outward and make wise decisions regarding clients. For example, if a client comes to us with a job that is clearly impossible and won't compromise on quotes or listen to our advice, they may not be a good fit.

How will you say no to prospects who don't fit your ideal customer profile?
We've always struggled with saying no. We need to avoid customers who don't really want help or a solution. They think they know what's best and just want the cheapest option. We're definitely not designed to serve everyone, but we struggle to say no because we need the revenue.

What is your "real currency" in business?

Right now we're focused on just getting things done, and we don't have a lot of consistency. Our currency is just getting the job done, but that doesn't have a lot of value.

What nonnegotiables do you need in place to ensure your clients trust you?

Consistent results, high quality, and empathy for their situation.

How do you build people-centric relationships with your clients?

We've already started to teach our team to think about each job as more than just a job. We need to look at the whole person and see the situation within the customer's paradigm.

Do you identify and solve clients' deeper problems? If not, what's preventing you from achieving this?

We are starting to! The new steps I put in place for initial calls and initial visits are already paying off.

How do you handle difficult conversations with clients or team members? What steps do you need to put in place to start handling these directly with empathy?

1. I need to focus more on empathy. Putting the person first will go a long way toward acting with empathy.

2. Some people on our team don't challenge others. We have to do both much better than we are. Our one-on-ones could be a key method of accomplishing this.

3. We need to reward feedback so others provide it regularly.

4. We need to lean into our value to serve our team.

How do you ensure that your business practices reflect your values and commitment to people?
I need to start by exemplifying my values more. Once I can do that consistently, I need to train my team and be transparent with them. I need to have them hold me accountable and vice versa. We need to develop a method to accomplish this through training and frequent communication. Already working on this!

Mentorship

What mentors have influenced your career and leadership style? Capture their best characteristics below. How can you emulate them?

- Bertha: She cared deeply about others and worked tirelessly for their success.

- Mom: She worked hard and consistently to do the most she could for her family.

Again, I need to ensure I put some consistency around my empathy. It has to be practiced and not just preached. I'm going to start by reminding myself of these every day. I'm going to ask my wife to hold me accountable.

How do you prioritize mentorship within your organization?
We don't, but we need to establish consistent coaching between an employee and their manager. I also want to meet with everyone periodically to ensure the culture is actually building.

Moving Forward

How can you apply these principles to improve your leadership and business practices?

- Discuss them with the team and at training sessions.

- Empower our team to identify the correct client profile.

- Continue equipping our team through training and practice to seek to understand our clients instead of just getting the job done. This includes listening and asking open-ended questions.

- Establish consistent internal touchpoints.

- Provide direct feedback quickly and simply. Reward it when it comes in.

Learn more about clients, mentorships, and business partners and download a blank, printable version of this worksheet at Scalable-BusinessFramework.com.

Chapter 7

Profit

"Hi, Barry!" Tim says, seeing Barry's now-familiar form striding up to the door of La Chance.

Barry turns around, beaming. "Hi, Tim," he says, swinging the door open. Three ladies in matching blue outfits walk out, thanking Barry as he waves Tim inside.

"After you," he says.

"Thanks." Tim walks in. The shop is still bedecked with Valentine's Day fare, and the two men get in line, peering at the menu. Tim smirks, pointing to a bizarre combo.

"How about we both try the Hot for Cupid? The espresso with honey and ... chili powder? That must be a special for Valentine's Day."

Barry raises an eyebrow. "You're on. But only if you try that whole-wheat vegan cheese tear-and-share."

Laughing, they place their orders, then loiter by the counter until the drinks arrive. Tim gives his a wary sniff.

"You first," Barry says. "This was your idea."

Tim takes a sip, grimacing. "Okay, I should have expected that kick at the end."

Barry tries his own drink and blinks, surprised. "Wow, that's . . . not as bad as I thought. Actually kind of good."

As the pair settles in at their usual table, Tim automatically draws out his folder, pulling out the worksheet.

"Ah, yes, the last people worksheet," Barry says, tearing off a piece of the bread. "Let's start with clients. What did you learn there?"

"Our current 'currency,'" Tim says with air quotes, "is just getting the job done because we're always in crisis mode. But it's inconsistent with our values. We need to focus on delivering solid results, maintaining high quality, and showing genuine empathy for our clients."

Barry eyes the worksheet, sniffing his piece of bread with its crumbly vegan cheese topping. "How will you build that trust and consistency?"

Tim pauses. "I think it starts with training the team to approach the work differently," he says. "And that's something I've already started to change. The team can see now that we're not just doing a job, and they're really trying to understand the client as a whole person. Uh, are you okay?"

Barry, who has taken a bite of his bread, seems to be choking. He grabs his coffee and takes a generous drink, then his eyes start bulging out of his head.

"Chili," he sputters, yanking a large water bottle out of his backpack and chugging as Tim watches, trying not to laugh.

"Well," Barry says in a hoarse voice, his eyes watering, "That vegan cheese is very... powdery. And a nice, big mouthful of chili flakes really washes it down nicely." He starts to wheeze with laughter, and Tim, unable to hold it in anymore, follows suit.

"Right," Barry says a minute later, wiping his eyes with a napkin. "It's all connected, isn't it? Living by your values trickles down into all aspects of business."

"Yes! Actually, we've already had a win I wanted to tell you about," Tim says.

Barry waves him ahead, going for another sip of water.

"After we talked about digging for the 'why' and a service-oriented approach, Sarah—she's one of my salespeople—noticed a particularly shy client hesitating when we asked about his priorities," Tim explains. "When she dug a little deeper, the client told us he was redoing his HVAC system because his son has severe asthma, and poor air quality was making the kid's condition worse. That changed everything. Knowing that, we were able to recommend specific solutions like UV lighting and advanced filtration systems tailored to their needs."

"That's amazing!" Barry exclaims. "That must have felt so gratifying."

"It really did," Tim says. "I can't wait to keep making changes."

"How about aligning your *clients* with your company's values and vision?" Barry asks, peering at the worksheet. "What's your approach there?"

Tim shuffles the worksheet to another section, trying to regain his focus. "Well, I think this is very different for Charis Strategies and FastTrack," he says. "I think we need to start internally. Once we're consistent in living out our values, we can train the team to recognize clients who *align* with those values. So, for example, a recalcitrant client who will clearly be impossible to please might not be a great fit."

Barry makes a face. "Do you generally accept those clients now?"

"Yeah, and it's not good," Tim admits. "Right before you and I started working together, we did an HVAC repair for this guy with a really old, shabby rental unit. Our techs got in there and found a bunch of rotted-out wood and moldering drywall. They told the client that he needed to replace a lot of the roof deck and even some of the ceiling joists, but he wouldn't listen and insisted we go ahead." Tim rubs his eyes. "They did, against their better judgment, and then guess what? The whole thing fell out of the ceiling four days later. Total nightmare. The guy had the gall to write us a negative review even after we gave him a refund."

Barry cringes. "That's tough. Making sure your clients are a good fit can definitely help you avoid those kinds of problems in the future."

"I hope so," Tim says. He feels his heart rate going up just thinking about that.

"Let's move on to mentorships," Barry says, eyeing Tim's expression. "What stood out to you there?"

Tim relaxes a little. "I thought about two key mentors in my life: Bertha and my mom. I need to be as consistently empathetic as they were— to practice it, not just preach it."

Barry smiles. "That's so crucial. And how will you make mentorship a priority at FastTrack?"

"We don't currently, but I want to establish consistent coaching between employees and their managers," Tim says. "We only have three team members in leadership roles, so it shouldn't be too hard to set up a meeting with them to discuss the new program and get their feedback. I also plan to meet at least annually with everyone myself to ensure we're actually building the culture we want."

Barry's eyes sparkle. "This is a strong plan, Tim. It's going to take time and effort, but if you stick with it, you'll see transformational results. Now, today, we're starting on the final P: profit."

Tim looks up. "Profit, huh? I like the sound of that." He gingerly tears off a piece of bread and starts brushing the vegan cheese off the top.

Barry grins. "I thought you might. You've brought it up a few times. And here's the thing: If your business isn't profitable, it's like this vegan cheese—something's just off."

Tim snorts. "I'll take your word for it," he says, and takes a cautious bite of the bread. It isn't half bad.

"At Charis Strategies, we view profit as a form of winning," Barry says in a dignified voice. "Profit enables us to grow, serve more clients, and create opportunities for our team. Without profitability, you won't be around long enough to make a difference."

Tim nods. "Right. Profit fuels the machine."

"Exactly," Barry says, taking another daring bite of his bread. "The second bite isn't nearly as bad, really."

"Glad you like it," Tim says, brushing more vegan cheese off his bread.

"If you're not profitable, you're just treading water," Barry says, waving his bread in the air. "Profit means you're not just keeping the lights on; you're creating the space to grow, to hire more people, and to actually fulfill the mission you started with."

Tim, typing some notes, says, "It makes sense. You need a solid financial base to support everything else."

Barry nods, and his tone grows a bit more serious. "Right. Some people think if you're mission-driven, you shouldn't care about profit. It's actually the opposite. Profit lets you take care of your team, reinvest, and keep pushing forward. It's what allows the mission to survive and thrive."

He leans back. "We're both entrepreneurs, and entrepreneurship is all about solving problems creatively. You see a barrier, and instead of giving up, you think, *How do I get through this?* Profit shows you're doing that efficiently. At Charis Strategies, we see profit as a measure that shows we're solving problems well. If we're not profitable, something's broken, and our business isn't going to last."

Tim nods, taking a thoughtful sip. "Profit ensures the business can stand the test of time while adding value."

"Absolutely," Barry says, leaning back in his chair. "Profit is a sign that you're solving problems efficiently while fulfilling your mission, and that's what entrepreneurship is all about."

Tim nods, typing this into his notes. "I couldn't agree more."

Barry grins, seizing a fork and unabashedly scraping vegan cheese off his bread. "Now, when people think about entrepreneurship, they often think it's all about coming up with the next big thing. But honestly, ideas are overrated."

Tim nods. "HVAC isn't exactly reinventing the wheel, I guess."

Having de-cheesed the bread, Barry takes a bite. "Much better," he says. "And you're exactly right. In today's culture, we glamorize the idea itself. We act like the concept is the most important part of the process. But in reality, what makes a business successful isn't the idea—it's the execution, the discipline, the intentional focus. That stuff might not sound sexy, but it's what makes you successful long term."

Tim pauses to think, nodding slowly. "Execution matters more than the idea itself?"

"Absolutely," Barry says without hesitation. "There's a big difference between inventors and entrepreneurs. Inventors create something new. Entrepreneurs, though, take that idea and turn it into something valuable—something people will actually pay for. A good idea doesn't automatically equal a good business. It's about how well you execute that makes the difference."

"Right," Tim says, typing, his hands dappled in sunlight from the wide windows. "So, a lot of people are putting their energy in the wrong place. They focus on the idea instead of figuring out how to make it work in the real world."

Barry grins. "Exactly. Thanks to shows like *Shark Tank*, people think having a great product means they're ready to run a business. But that's not the case. You could have the best idea in the world, but if you can't build a sustainable model around it, it's not going to last. Most successful businesses aren't even built on entirely new ideas."

"I guess that's true," Tim says. "We mostly need and want the things we already know."

Barry nods. "That's right. Look at Apple—they didn't invent the computer, the smartphone, or vision goggles. They just took existing concepts and made them better. They didn't need a brand-new idea. They just had to execute better than anyone else."

Tim licks a bit of remaining vegan cheese off his bread, then grimaces and puts it down.

"Uber is another great example," Barry says. "They didn't invent the taxi, but they took that concept and completely transformed it. They created a whole new marketplace by improving on what was already there."

Tim nods, grabbing a knife to scrape more vegan cheese off his bread. "That makes sense. But breaking into a market in an unconventional way, like Uber did, must've been tough."

"It was," Barry says. "Uber faced all kinds of challenges—legal issues, financial struggles, operational hurdles. It took a lot of money, persistence, and grit to disrupt an established industry.[23] But their gamble did pay off in the end. Most businesses can focus on small-scale improvements rather than trying to create a whole new niche. It's usually a more sustainable path to success."

Tim smiles. "That seems much more attainable than inventing some life-changing creation."

"As for improving instead of reinventing," Barry says, "entrepreneur and author Scott Belsky put it perfectly: 'Ideas are cheap and abundant, but what's valuable is effectively placing those ideas into situations that develop into action.'[24] You need innovative ideas, sure. But then you need the ability to execute them in the marketplace."

Tim leans back. "That's a good reminder. You have to be able to execute on the idea." The door to La Chance swings open, letting in a cool gust of air and a group of people in business suits.

Barry smiles. "Success is all about execution. That's the difference between people who succeed and those who just dream."

---

23 "The Rise and Challenges of Uber: A Story of Disruption and Innovation," *The Brand Hopper* (blog), May 1, 2023, https://thebrandhopper.com/2023/05/01/the-rise-and-challenges-of-uber-a-story-of-disruption-and-innovation.

24 Scott Belsky, *Making Ideas Happen: Overcoming the Obstacles Between Vision and Reality* (Penguin Books Ltd., 2011), 4.

Tim leans forward. "So, how do you make sure your business stands out in the market? How do you make it unique?"

Barry grins. "Good question. Here's the thing about uniqueness—it's really all about how the customer perceives it. If the customer thinks what you're offering is unique, then it is. Look at Apple again. They're masters at making people feel like what they're offering is special. Perception becomes reality."

Tim nods. "Make the customer feel like what you're offering is different," he repeats.

Barry continues. "Those differences can come from the value you're adding to the marketplace. Once you have that, you can keep iterating and innovating, which makes your product or service feel distinct. Often that sense of uniqueness is just a mindset—the customer thinks it's different, and that's what matters. Take jeans, for example. Lots of companies make them, but people have their favorite brands and think they're unlike any other. It's easy to copy a product; it's much harder to copy that brand perception. That's where branding comes into play."

Tim smiles. "Okay, yeah. This is starting to make sense."

"Great," Barry says, taking another piece of bread and scraping the last of the vegan cheese off. "And once you've proven you have a solid solution, it's about building a sustainable business model around it."

Tim leans in again, taking another piece of the tear-and-share. "Okay. What do you mean by a sustainable business model?"

Barry smiles. "It's one that's repeatable and built on consistent systems that deliver real value to customers. It ensures those customers will keep coming back and referring your products and services to other people over the long term, which leads to long-term profits and keeps the business healthy." He takes a bite as though to punctuate the point.

Tim is still processing everything. His brow furrows. "So, the key isn't just making a profit today. It's setting up a system that keeps delivering value and making money over the long term?"

Barry nods, leaning back. "Exactly. That's the secret sauce—building a business model around your product or solution so that the market votes with their dollars and keeps paying for it. That way, you can turn a profit over time. At Charis Strategies, we look at profitability as a measure of how well we're solving problems and adding value over the long term. We want to build something customers don't just want once but keep coming back for."

Tim smiles, feeling the pieces click together. "Building something that lasts and keeps adding value."

"Right," Barry agrees. "As management theory titan Peter Drucker said, 'Profit is not the purpose of a business, but rather the test of its validity.'[25] Without profit, you won't have the resources to keep improving and delivering value to your customers."

Tim's fingers fly over the keys as he types. "So," he asks, "can we make this more specific to my situation? How do I make people think FastTrack is unique? The HVAC market is huge. I've got quite a bit of competition, and it can get overwhelming."

Barry nods, dusting bread crumbs off his hands, then waving to someone. Tim turns to see that it's the businesspeople from earlier, headed back out of the shop.

"Great question," Barry says to Tim. "It starts with understanding your market, what we call your total addressable market, or TAM for short. Investors talk about this concept a lot. It's basically about how big the market for your product or service is."

Tim picks up his coffee. "Right, I've heard that before. So, bigger is better?"

"In general, yes," Barry says. "With a big market, you don't have to grab as much market share to make good money. The larger the market, the more room there is for profit. At Charis Strategies, we've seen that bigger markets offer more opportunities to scale, but they also come with more competition—more people fighting for the same customers."

---

25 Peter Drucker, *Management: Tasks, Responsibilities, Practices* (Harper & Row, 1974), 79.

Tim nods. "That's why investors care so much about market size—it lowers their risk."

"Exactly," Barry continues. "With a big market, you've got more room for error. You can mess up a few things and still make it work because the opportunity is huge. But if you're going after a small niche, you need to be really careful. Even if you're amazing at what you do, if the market's too small, you won't make enough money to keep the business going. You might have the best product in the world, but if there aren't enough people to buy it, you're stuck."

Tim presses his lips together, thinking. "I feel like that bodes well for me, at least once I've got my act together enough to scale. Everyone needs HVAC."

"Definitely," Barry says, smiling. "Investor Peter Lynch has this great quote: 'Go for a business that any idiot can run—because sooner or later any idiot probably is going to be running it.'[26] That's how investors think; they know execution is tough, so they want a big enough market to cushion the mistakes. At the same time, you want that sweet spot, a market big enough for you to add value and capture enough share to build a solid business. At Charis Strategies, we've learned that profitability comes from finding that balance. But you also need to keep competition in check. It's like finding the golden ticket for business leaders."

Tim nods. "Okay. Let's think about FastTrack for a second. There are a few ways I can expand my market if I want to really have as much opportunity as possible. I can

---

26 "Track Companies, Not Markets," *USA Today*, March 7, 1989, 4B.

send techs out in a wider radius, or I can expand the services I offer. But you told me when we started working together that I needed to hold off on expansion until I had a solid foundation in place."

Barry nods, cradling his mug in both hands as the espresso machine lets out a loud squeal behind the counter. "Yes, that's true. But you've already done a lot of work to strengthen your foundation. Once we really get into the Scalable Business Framework in the next few weeks, you can go ahead and resume work on expanding sustainably to increase your reach."

"Hey, that's great," Tim says.

"That being said, you have to be very careful when adding new services," Barry says. "A lot of entrepreneurs get distracted and want to branch out into other things, but once you find what's working, you've got to have the discipline to stick with it."

Tim stops typing and looks at Barry. "How so?"

"Once your business model is gaining traction, *focus* becomes critical," Barry says. "As you implement these changes, you will likely start making more sales even without adding services."

"Yeah, that's true," Tim says.

"Well, you need to keep adding value and executing well without getting sidetracked by shiny new ideas that may not turn out to be good for business," Barry says. "The key is balancing market opportunity with focus and making sure you're not spreading yourself too thin."

Barry puts his palms up and bobbles them up and down, representing a scale. "It's all about balance—capturing enough market share while staying focused and disciplined enough to avoid distractions. That's where sustainable growth comes from."

Tim types, then slumps back in his chair and sighs. He looks up at Barry. "That all sounds like a delicate balance to strike. What if things don't go as planned? How do you know when to pivot or when to keep pushing?"

Barry leans forward, smiling. "That's when you want to fail fast. If you're entering a competitive market and think you've got something unique, or at least something customers think is unique, test it quickly. Validate your assumptions early. You don't want to spend years only to find out your idea isn't as great as you thought."

Tim nods. "So, you're saying it's better to fail fast and pivot quickly than to drag it out? I've never thought about it that way before."

"It's not the usual mindset, but I think it works well," Barry says, bending down to pick up a napkin that has fluttered to the floor.

"I don't like obsessing over the competition, but when you're starting out, you need to know what they're doing," Barry says, putting the crumpled napkin on the edge of the table. "If your competitors have deep pockets, they can outspend and outlast you, even if your solution is better."

Tim ponders this. "So, even if you have the best solution, they can still win because they have more resources? I don't like the sound of that."

Barry sighs, glancing into his coffee cup, then taking a sip. "Unfortunately, yes. Also, I think this coffee is getting spicier." He smacks his lips, grabs his water bottle, and takes a sip before continuing. "If other companies have more capital, they can outlast you. At Charis Strategies, we've seen how winning in terms of profitability doesn't always mean having the best product—it's just about making sure your business can survive and compete. That's why testing your idea quickly is so important. If it can't compete, you need to pivot before you run out of cash."

Tim can see the logic in this. "As soon as cash flow dries up, it's game over."

Barry nods. "Absolutely. Cash is everything. One of the biggest mistakes I see is entrepreneurs not fully grasping how important cash flow is. If you can't generate cash flow and profit, your business is in trouble. Cash gives you flexibility—it lets you make smart decisions and survive tough times."

Tim lifts himself from his slouched position and starts typing again. "What happens if you're trying to make changes, but you're not generating the cash flow you expected?"

"That's when things get tough," Barry explains. "You'll have to figure out how to raise money or, worse, start taking personal risks like mortgaging your house. That's why becoming cash flow positive as soon as possible is vital. Dave Ramsey said, 'A business is something that makes you money. If you're not making money, it's a hobby.'[27] If you're not making a profit, it's not sustainable."

Tim nods. "And it's an expensive, boring hobby at that."

"Running out of cash is the number one reason businesses fail," Barry says. "That's why managing cash flow is critical."

He pauses to swig down the last of his coffee. "Oh, wow," he says, shuddering. "Lots of chili powder down there. Skip that last sip, Tim, if you haven't made that mistake already."

Tim laughs. "Will do. Want a palate cleanser? I'm buying."

"Would you get me a mint tea?" Barry says, grabbing his water bottle. "We do have a few more things to discuss."

"Sure thing," Tim says, still chuckling as he rises. A few minutes later, he's back with two steaming mint teas.

"Oh, that's so much better," Barry says gratefully after his first large sip. "Thank you."

"Anytime," Tim says. "I guess we're not so Hot for Cupid after all."

---

27 Megan McArdle, "Dave Ramsey Talks About His New Book," *The Atlantic*, September 23, 2011, https://www.theatlantic.com/personal/archive/2011/09/dave-ramsey-talks-about-his-new-book/244027.

"Apparently not," Barry says, looking pensive. "It was still fun to try something new, though. I wonder what they'll have for Easter . . ."

"Too soon," Tim says, laughing. "So, um, we were talking about—" he scans his notes. "Cash flow. Manage your cash flow, test your assumptions, and don't be afraid to pivot quickly—that's the key. That makes me think . . . I'm guessing businesses that need a lot of capital up front, like aviation or real estate, face different challenges than service-based ones."

Barry nods. "Oh, yes. Capital-intensive businesses require significant up-front investment. You need to manage cash flow carefully until you can start generating revenue. Service-based businesses, like consulting, can generate cash faster because you get paid for the hours you work. At Charis Strategies, we've seen this firsthand, but service-based businesses come with their own challenges—like limited opportunities for recurring revenue compared to product-based businesses."

Tim nods. "So, depending on the business type, your approach to cash flow management needs to be different. HVAC isn't as expensive as some businesses, but it isn't cheap either."

"Right," Barry says. "No matter what kind of business you have, cash flow is your lifeline. Without it, even the best ideas will fail."

Tim absently bobs his teabag around in his cup, then removes it and places it on his saucer as he mulls this over.

"I know I'm not a new business owner," Tim says, "But I'm kind of wondering: How do new entrepreneurs balance risk? Getting a new venture off the ground is often the hardest part. I never had to do that, but I might want to in the future, you know?"

"Sure," Barry says. "For new businesses, I'm not a fan of going all-in right from the start. People often think entrepreneurs are huge risk-takers, but we're more calculated. We bet on ourselves, and I'd much rather bet on myself than rely on corporate America or a big job. But even so, a new business owner doesn't have to quit their day job or mortgage their house to get started. Someone working on expanding their business, like you, is in the same boat. You can test things out, prove the concept, and still have the flexibility to pivot if they need to. You're committed, but you're not in so deep that you can't turn back."

Tim takes a sip of tea, enjoying the strong, minty flavor. "So, start small before taking the full leap?"

"Exactly," Barry says. "Position yourself to prove a few key things first—like whether there's a market for your new service or whether you can overcome certain challenges. You don't need to invest a lot of capital up front or take on too much risk before knowing if it's going to work."

Tim thinks for a moment, then begins to type as Barry keeps talking.

"At some point, you'll need to commit fully, but don't rush it," Barry says. "Don't take big risks before proving some key things along the way. Here's an example: I helped start a nonprofit called Blue Hill Grace. We provide housing for families who come to Birmingham for medical care. We give them a place to stay when they're away from home for transplants, cancer treatments, or other serious medical needs."

Tim's eyes widen. "That's incredible! How did you get started?"

Barry smiles. "At first, we planned to build or buy a building with rooms for families. But that was capital-intensive, and we didn't have any capital. Plus, we hadn't even proven the model."

"So, what did you do instead?" Tim asks, leaning his elbow on the table and cupping his chin.

"We pivoted to an apartment model," Barry explains. "One of the founders owned a couple of apartments, so we furnished them and started working with hospitals to bring in patients. We tested the logistics and proved the concept without investing millions up front. Once we knew it worked, we added more apartments and scaled up."

"Nice," says Tim. "That's smart."

"Exactly," Barry agrees. "Once we proved the model worked, we could grow quickly. Blue Hill Grace has thrived for over ten years now. If we had tried to build or buy a building from the start, we might never have gotten off the ground—or we might have failed because of the huge up-front costs."

Tim smiles. "So, the key is to get started without taking too much risk—prove the concept, then scale."

"Right," Barry says, patting the table in front of him. "Start small, prove the concept, and *then* get bigger. It's a more sustainable way to build a business or run an existing one. You don't have to go all-in from day one. Once you know the market is there and the idea works, then you can grow with confidence."

"So," Tim says, "I'm guessing there's a worksheet that'll help me think through some of this."

"Sure is," Barry says. "The worksheet will help you distill what drives profit in your market into a single principle. It's waiting in your inbox. But before you go, I've got one last little anecdote for you. Ever heard of Matthew Emmons?"

Tim shakes his head, reaching for his mug.

"He's a well-known American rifle shooter who's won multiple Olympic medals," Barry explains. "Back in the 2004 Athens Olympics, he was in his final heat, leading the competition by a wide margin—practically unbeatable. He approached his final target, controlled his breathing, aimed just like he'd done countless times before, pulled the trigger, and hit the bullseye. But when he looked up, he realized he had hit the *wrong* bullseye—his competitor's target. That one mistake cost him the gold, dropping him from first to eighth place."[28]

Tim whistles softly, and Barry leans in closer.

"We all have a scoreboard, Tim. Matthew Emmons had one, but he aimed for the target that didn't affect that

---

[28] "Matthew Emmons and His Bittersweet Memories of the Olympic Games," Olympics.com, August 23, 2020, https://olympics.com/en/news/matthew-emmons-and-his-bittersweet-memories-of-the-olympic-games.

scoreboard. Are you aiming for the right target—the one that's relevant to your score? To me, it's better to lose on the right scoreboard than to win on the wrong one."

Tim nods slowly.

"This applies to everything, but I think it's very applicable to profit in this case," Barry says. "Everything at Charis Strategies has been built with intentionality and focus. I'm okay with failing, but I'm not going to build a business I don't like and love, and I'm not going to build one that doesn't align with my purpose or that isn't capable of self-sustaining through profit."

Tim nods. "I get that," he says.

The two men start putting away their things and pulling on their jackets.

"So, this was the last day for the Three P's, huh?" Tim asks. "Have I graduated?"

"Do you feel like you've graduated?" Barry asks, shouldering his gym bag.

"Definitely not," Tim says with a laugh. "I've learned so much, but I think I've got a ways to go."

"Yes," Barry says. "Consider the Three P's prerequisites for what's coming. I think you're really going to enjoy our conversation next week."

Chapter 7 Summary

The Three P's: Profit

Profitability and Growth
- Profit is essential to business survival and growth.
- A strong financial foundation supports all other business aspects.
- A sustainable business model delivers consistent value.
- Long-term profitability depends on steady, reliable operations.

Execution over Ideas
- Executing your idea is more important than just having an idea.
- Improving existing concepts is often a more successful approach than creating something entirely new.

Business Considerations and Approach
- Consider market size and competition.
- Align business with personal values and purpose.
- Ensure effective cash flow management.
- Test ideas quickly and be ready to pivot when necessary.
- Recognize risks of rapid expansion; balance risk by starting small to prove a concept before scaling.

Profit Worksheet

In building a great company, there is no single defining action, no grand program, no one killer innovation, no solitary lucky break, no miracle moment. Rather, the process resembles relentlessly pushing a giant, heavy flywheel, turn upon turn, building momentum until a point of breakthrough, and beyond.
—**Jim Collins**[29]

There's no quick trick to turn your purpose into profit. However, you will need a plan to start. Let's unpack what profit looks like for your team, who your customer should be, and how you can begin to turn the flywheel. At the end of the worksheet, you'll be asked to identify your profit principle based on the answers below.

---

29 Jim Collins, *Good to Great: Why Some Companies Make the Leap . . . and Others Don't* (Harper Business, 2001), 165.

Define the Win

> *Profit is not the purpose of a business, but rather the test of its validity.*
> —**Peter Drucker**[30]

What does winning look like for your company? Be specific.
- Customer is happy and peace is restored.

- We solved the problem the right way and explained all options to the customer.

- We made a reasonable profit on the individual job.

What is your scoreboard? How will you know you're winning?
- Client satisfaction metric

- Net margin per job

What key factors will ensure your business makes a profit?
- A consistent methodology and process so all employees do things the same way and every customer gets a consistent experience

---

30 Drucker, *Management*, 79.

- A clear outline of all options and prices for customers (get them to sign off on options and price before we do work)

- Clear checklists and manuals to solve common problems (a clear playbook)

- Defined employee training and development to upskill and develop our team

- Minimal travel time per job

- Minimal time between jobs

What processes are you missing to track these?
We're pretty much missing all the processes we need right now ...

Tip: Figuring out the key drivers (inputs) that produce the right outcomes (profit) for your business is an iterative process. Try to test, stay consistent, and don't over-engineer processes until you know they work. Then measure and learn from your mistakes.

Identify the Customer

How do your ideal customers recognize your value and pay you based on the value you provide (versus price)?

As the saying goes, "Quality, Speed, and Price — you pick two." We will deliver a better overall experience, with better results, in a timelier manner than the client expects.

How do you build a meaningful relationship with your customers so they don't view your service/product as a transaction?

Overcommunication and transparency. Communicate before, during, and after the job in a way that builds trust.

Have you confirmed that your ideal customers will pay you? Cash on hand is the only way to validate your business as real because customers vote with their dollars, not their intentions.

We need to be up front about the cost. We might even need to start charging for the initial diagnosis and trip out.

Work the Plan

A business that doesn't generate a profit consistently over time is a hobby, not a business.
—**Dave Ramsey**[31]

How will you ensure you deliver services/products to your ideal customers that make a profit and differentiate you from your competitors?

> Part of our one focus is <u>getting it right the first time</u>. There are only two ways to do something: right or again. That means correct diagnosis, correct parts, and correct installation with no confusion and no room for error.
>
> We need to lean on <u>strong process documentation</u> so that anyone on our team can accomplish any repair and installation more efficiently than our competitors. This means we plan our routes and schedules out to make the most effective use of our team's time. We also have all the right parts for that day on the trucks so there is no time lost in repair.

---

31   McArdle, "Dave Ramsey Talks About His New Book."

How will you ensure you stay aligned with your purpose and people core principles while you generate profit?

Purpose: If we accomplish our purpose and truly bring peace, that's worth more than a budget repair from a competitor.

People: If our team truly _serves_ each other, we have everything we need for every job (parts, schedule, and knowledge) because the whole team works together to make it happen. This minimizes costs and lets us charge more for our services, and the customer also ultimately saves because they get a quality service that won't require as much maintenance down the line. That maximizes profit and aligns with our purpose.

How will you ensure you don't become greedy and focus too much on profit and not enough on purpose and people? How will you stay aligned and hold yourself and the company accountable?

If we focus too much on the _one_ job (profit principle), we violate our peace principle because it's about the customer.

If we focus too much on the _one_ job (profit principle), we sacrifice the team's ability to serve their teammates because we become self-serving.

The focus on peace and serving helps us balance our one job focus for profit.

What incentive plans will you put in place to keep your people focused on the key drivers of the business so the business remains profitable over the long term?

The question is, how do we incentivize creating peace for our clients, serving each other, and focusing on one job at a time?

- *We can roll all of this into a compensation plan for techs. They make a commission on the margin for each job, which incentivizes profit.*

- *To balance that, their bonus payout will fall based on average reviews. If they average below 4.5/5 over a rolling six months, they won't get their bonus.*

- *Finally, we'll pay a bonus to each team that hits their profit goals.*

How will you avoid making rash, unwise decisions when times are difficult? Think about how your purpose and people are impacted here.

I think meeting consistently with our leadership team would help me balance my decision-making. I need to empower them and have them brought into our purpose and people. They can help counsel me and make the best decisions. If we keep those values in mind, we will be successful.

Tip: Once you figure out what works, develop processes to ensure consistency, repeatability, and scalability.

Profit

What is your profit principle and why? **(Fill this out last)**

One job at a time is our focus. Every job matters to us. Every job is an opportunity to make a customer happy, solve their problem the right way, and make a profit. Happy customers refer us to other good customers. It's a cycle that allows us to grow while continuing to make a profit so we have a sustainable business in the long term. While we aren't perfect, our goal is to do this for <u>every single</u> job. We focus on <u>one</u> job at a time. Over time, this builds a successful, sustainable company that makes money.

Learn more about profit and download a
blank, printable version of this worksheet at
ScalableBusinessFramework.com.

Part 3

The Scalable Business Framework

Chapter 8

Strategic Objectives

When Tim bursts into La Chance the following Tuesday, the Valentine's Day decorations are still up—hearts and red ribbons hang near the windows. Barry waves him over to a table already laden with mugs and plates.

"Already got you covered," he says.

"Hey, thanks." Tim shrugs out of his jacket. "What did you get?" He points to the steaming mug on the table.

"Your usual," Barry says. "I also bought a couple of walnut bars. They're delicious and made for health-conscious folks."

"That was nice of you," Tim says as he slips into his seat and takes out his laptop. "Not a fan of the vegan bread, huh?"

Barry laughs. "I try to stay healthy."

"I've noticed." Tim rolls his eyes as he opens up his notes and seizes a walnut bar.

"Hey, now," Barry says. "You're already looking a little more energetic than you did when we first met."

"Actually," Tim says, "I *have* been getting in a little bit of physical activity. I got myself a walking pad for my office. It's not amazing, but it's better than sitting on my butt all day. And now that I'm home at a decent hour, I can play with my kids to get some movement in, and I've mostly stopped downing piles of junk food at work. I've already lost seven pounds!"

"That's wonderful!" Barry says. "As we continue working together, you may find you have even more time to dedicate to exercise and healthy eating if that's what you want to do. Not to mention other activities. Did you get to do something nice for your wife for Valentine's Day?"

"Yeah," Tim says. "I actually *made it* to our dinner reservation this year. I had to bail on her for several years before due to emergencies, but this year I made a point to leave it all and just go."

"Excellent," Barry says. "Now, let's get down to business. Tim, how did your homework go?"

Tim nods, savoring the rich flavors of honey and cinnamon in his walnut bar. "Really well. Wow, this bar is really good."

Barry smiles. "It's my go-to when they have it."

"Might be mine now, too," Tim says, pulling out his worksheet. He sets the crisp pages on the table between them.

"Well, looks like you've done some solid thinking," Barry says, his eyes darting over the page. "You said winning means having happy customers, solving their problems the right way, and making a reasonable profit on each job. That's a strong start. You've identified the key drivers of your business—consistent processes, clear communication with customers, training for your team, and minimal travel time between jobs. Those are the levers you can pull to make profit predictable."

Barry flips to the next section. "You've got a clear idea of your ideal customer too—a homeowner who's stressed about a broken HVAC system and worried about costs. You're in the right spot there. And I like that you're focused on getting the job done right the first time. 'One' is an excellent profit principle for FastTrack."

"Correct diagnosis, correct parts, correct installation," Tim rattles off. "I've always liked thinking about efficiency that way. Oh, I also wanted to circle back to some of the other changes I've been making."

"Sure," Barry says. "I'd love to hear about it."

"I decided to hold a little in-office retreat day," Tim says. "We all took the morning off to have a company-wide meeting, and all we did was discuss the new vision and culture changes. I actually had some key ideas—our vision and mission statement, the Three P directives—printed off on posters that I put in a couple of places in the office. I gave some time for feedback and discussion, and then, during the afternoon, we had breakout sessions for managers to start coaching."

"Wow!" Barry says, his eyes widening. "That sounds amazing. How did it go?"

"Really well," Tim says. "My three managers were all really excited about it. We've already started making changes, so it didn't come out of the blue. Since you and I had already finished discussing the Three P's, I was anxious to establish all these new ideas company-wide, so we're all on the same page."

"And everyone seemed okay with it?" Barry asks.

"I did get some pushback from a few people, but almost everyone seemed pretty on board," Tim says. "They especially liked it when I announced a flex work-from-home schedule option for employees whose jobs don't rely on proximity." He laughs.

Barry chuckles. "Yes, I can see how they would have liked that. What are you going to do about the naysayers?"

"I scheduled one-on-ones with them," Tim says. "Most of them were just nervous about the changes. One of them, though, I think I may have to let go. I'm gonna try one more meeting with him first, after he's had some time to think."

Barry nods as the hiss of the milk frother fills the shop. "Like we said, if they don't align with the new culture, sometimes you do have to make hard calls like that. Despite a few growing pains, it's so great that you're taking steps to change your company culture. The question now is how to make all these big business goals happen."

Barry claps his hands. "You've identified your Three P's, including your purpose. Now the key is to maintain focus and keep yourself aligned. On life's journey, you're going to end up somewhere no matter what. Identifying your purpose is a massive first step down the right path. But it's rare to get to a destination intentionally unless you stay intentional about it. You've got to keep checking your map, looking for landmarks, and correcting course."

Steepling his fingers, Barry leans forward. "I want all of us to end up there on purpose. That's why, once you've defined your 'why,' the next step is to stay focused and aligned. That's really what I want to talk about today—maintaining purpose by creating goals and milestones."

Tim types some of this into his notes doc. "Okay. That makes a lot of sense."

"Now, I know we ended our Three P's discussion last week," Barry says. "But I wanted to quickly tie it all together, because I think that will give you a good frame of reference for today's conversation. The Three P's—purpose, people, and profit—form the core of a successful business, but only when they work together."

Tim types furiously as Barry, sitting back and crossing one leg over the other, continues to talk.

"Think of it like this: Purpose, people, and profit are three vital forces in a dynamic equilibrium—like planets exerting gravitational pull on one another. When these forces are properly balanced, they create a stable orbit for your business to thrive. Purpose provides direction, people deliver value, and profit ensures sustainability. However, if any one force dominates or weakens, the entire system is thrown into disarray."

Barry gestures with one hand. "Take profit, for example. If we're not profitable, we can't stay in business to serve our clients. But profit is only part of the equation. If we overwork or underpay our employees, we lose them. And if we don't have enough people to serve our clients, we fail to deliver value."

Tim narrows his eyes as he visualizes the concept. "So you have to balance the three to keep the business functioning properly."

Barry nods. "Right. The art of leadership lies in maintaining this delicate balance, understanding that these forces simultaneously reinforce and challenge one another in a constant dance of healthy tension. That's when you create a flywheel effect—once it starts spinning, it builds momentum. I've got a great Jim Collins quote about this. Hang on . . ."

He opens his phone and touches the screen a few times. "Here we go. This is from his book *Turning the Flywheel*: 'In building a great company, there is no single defining action. . . . Rather, the process resembles relentlessly pushing a giant, heavy flywheel, turn upon turn, building momentum until a point of breakthrough, and beyond.'[32] In other words, the more aligned everything is, the more sustainable the growth becomes."

Tim leans back, a smile spreading across his face. "I see it. That alignment keeps the business moving forward, always gaining momentum."

"Exactly," Barry says. "When you've got a clear purpose, you focus on your people, and you maintain a healthy profit, you can address issues quickly before they spiral into bigger problems."

Tim thinks it over. "So, when profit, people, and purpose are all aligned, you're not just running the business—you're scaling it. I like that."

"What's not to like?" Barry says with a laugh. "When the Three P's are balanced, they support each other. Profit keeps you financially stable, people drive the growth, and purpose gives you direction. If any of those get out of sync, the whole system wobbles. But when they're aligned, the business becomes resilient and adaptable, able to handle challenges and keep moving forward."

"Right," says Tim. "I can definitely see how keeping those three aligned would make a business much more adaptable and sustainable."

Barry smiles. "Now, let me ask you a question. Up until now, what have your goals and objectives been at FastTrack?"

---

32 Jim Collins, *Turning the Flywheel: A Monograph to Accompany "Good to Great"* (Penguin Random House, 2019).

"Not crashing and burning," Tim admits with a laugh. "But after the past month, I think I'm starting to get it. I really do. It's about making the *right* kind of progress—the kind that keeps me aligned with my purpose, which is helping people get something they need at a good value. And, ultimately, that should lead to a more profitable business."

Barry leans back. "That's exactly it, Tim. For example, at Charis Strategies, our BHAG, as Jim Collins would call it,[33] is to be a blessing at scale."

"BHAG?"

"Big, hairy, audacious goal," Barry says with a chuckle.

"That's memorable." Tim laughs.

"Very catchy," Barry agrees. "I chose 'Being a blessing at scale' as our BHAG—our vision, basically—because very few businesses have gotten bigger and kept their culture. It's hard to stay true to who you are as you grow. Lots of businesses sell their soul and stop being who they wanted to be."

"I can see that being a challenge," Tim says. "So, my vision—the one I already came up with—can serve as my BHAG? To serve people with excellence?"

"You bet," Barry says. "The BHAG is the overarching theme, and it helps guide a lot of your other goals. Those start with strategic objectives."

Tim creates a new heading as Barry explains.

---

[33] James C. Collins and Jerry I. Porras, *Built to Last: Successful Habits of Visionary Companies* (Random House Business Books, 2005).

"Every year at Beacon, Charis Strategies, and the other businesses I contribute to, we identify two or three strategic objectives to concentrate on," Barry says. "These strategic objectives need to align with all Three P's. You can't focus solely on purpose and neglect your people or the business's profitability. That's how you grow while staying balanced. The Three P's are like your North Star, keeping everything aligned."

"That's why we had to start there," Tim says.

"Exactly," Barry says, picking up his mug. "I always use the Three P's, even when taking on new projects. That's why you and I spent so much time on them. They're absolutely foundational to a successful business in my opinion. Every time I start a new project, I ask myself: Will this accomplish our purpose? How will it impact our people? And will it allow us to make a profit?"

Barry traces a triangle in the air with one finger. "It's like a triangle. You have to have all three sides, and you can't sacrifice one. So when you think about goals, always run them through this framework. If it aligns with all Three P's, then it's a good goal."

Tim stops typing and takes a contemplative sip of his coffee. "That's great," he says. "I'm feeling really good about my Three P's thanks to all the work we did on them, so I think I'm in a good place to assess whether my objectives line up with them."

"Excellent," Barry replies. "So, once you've outlined your Three P's, the next step is to set strategic objectives to achieve them. Later on, we'll dive into the Scalable Business Framework, which will be more detailed. Right now we're focusing on the high-level concepts."

"Fine with me," Tim says, taking another bite of his walnut bar. "I know you won't give me answers about my own strategic objectives, but can you give me a frame of reference by filling me in on the ones you use at Charis Strategies?"

"Absolutely," Barry says. "This year, we have three main strategic objectives: growing outbound sales, improving client retention, and developing our processes and systems for the next level of growth."

"So you're pretty seriously working on scaling at this point," Tim muses.

"Yes," Barry says. "Here's another example: A few years ago, we decided to start working with a new CRM. I tend to phrase strategic objectives as questions, and that year, the main question was, 'Can we implement another platform, and does it make sense for our business?' So our focus was on diversifying the software we implemented. If it worked, great; if not, we had to either commit or move on. Luckily, it ended up working really well."

"I like the idea of phrasing these as questions," Tim says. "Somehow it makes them feel less daunting."

"I feel the same way," Barry says. "Each year, we aim to answer key questions like, 'Can we do this?' or 'Does this make sense?' Then we set our goals and start implementing with the framework to answer the question."

Tim ponders this, munching a second walnut bar. "I'm guessing the types of objectives you have change as your business evolves?"

"Oh, yes," Barry says. "Let me give you a snapshot of how these goals have evolved over time. Ten years ago, my main objective was to prove that Charis Strategies was a real business. The question was simply, 'Is this a real business?'" He lets out a little laugh. "Turns out it was. The next year, the focus was, 'What do we really do?' That year, we solidified our focus of tailoring our services around a CRM platform and stopped trying to do everything for everyone."

"I like how you use the strategic objective questions to guide your evolution," Tim says, starting to wonder what questions he needs to answer about FastTrack. "That's very smart."

"It works well for me," Barry says, shrugging. "Eight years ago, the goal was to build a team to do the work so it wasn't just me doing everything. By the next year, the question became, 'Can we scale it? Could we grow from twenty to forty to sixty people?'"

Barry takes a breath. "Three years ago, we scaled up to over sixty employees, serving the entire US, and even explored acquisition opportunities," he says. "That year, we acquired a small company—that was one of our goals. These kinds of questions and goals have driven our growth. We keep it simple: two or three strategic objectives a year that align with our Three P's." He stops. "Why are you laughing?"

"I'm just impressed that you could rattle all those off like that, even the ones from years ago," Tim says. "I can't even remember what I had for breakfast this morning."

Barry lets out a small chuckle. "Yes, well, I spent so much time thinking about those objectives that they wormed their way into my brain. Did you notice a pattern with the objectives over time, by any chance?"

Tim ponders this. "The early years were more binary," he says finally. "'Is this a real business?' and 'Can we scale?' are fairly simple queries. But as you grew, the objectives evolved in complexity and size."

"Bingo," Barry says happily. "That's where having a clear purpose, along with the Three P's, has helped us keep everything in alignment. Now, Tim, let's test that bad memory of yours. Do you remember when we talked about failing fast last week?"

"Yeah, I do, actually," Tim says. "That was part of our profit discussion. You said it's better to fail and pivot than to spend a long time on a bad idea."

"Right," Barry affirms. "And that's a key reason I phrase these strategic goals as questions. The answer is usually either yes or no. Asking the question lets you succeed or fail fast. If the question is, 'Will my business scale?' and the answer is no, you can learn that fairly quickly without wasting four or five years to realize the business won't scale. This creates a sense of urgency. And honestly, it's okay if the answer is no. It's just important to find out quickly and learn from it."

"Okay," Tim said slowly. "I get that. Even if the answer to the strategic objective question is no, it doesn't mean your business is doomed or anything. You just have to pivot."

"Precisely," Barry says, toasting Tim with his mug. "The sooner you realize it's not working, the sooner you can adapt, evolve, and move on. You won't waste time figuring it out later."

"Hmm," Tim says, leaning back. "It kind of reminds me of poker."

Barry cocks his head. "How so?"

"In poker, you have to bet to stay in a hand to win it, but the main purpose of betting is to gain insight as you won't win every hand," Tim says, working through the comparison as he talks. "When you place a bet, your goal is to gain information about the other players and their hands so you can decide if you want to stay in or fold. Worst case, your bet allows you to learn something about the other players that you can use in future hands. Best case, you win!"

"That's a great analogy!" Barry says. "A good poker player uses betting as a way to gather information. I view setting milestones and objectives in the same way. We're essentially making a bet, and then spending real money, time, and resources to get information. Yes, we hope to win, but even if we don't, we've gained valuable insights that will help us win in the future."

"Okay," Tim says, "this is starting to really make sense."

"Now, once you've got strategic objectives that align with your purpose, you've got to divide them up some more,"

Barry says. He picks up a walnut bar and holds it aloft in a weak pool of winter sunlight. In the background, Tim hears the quiet strains of jazz piano through La Chance's speakers; the café isn't very crowded today.

"If I tried to eat this whole thing in one bite without chewing it, I'd probably end up in the ER," Barry says. "But if I break it up into pieces and remember to chew it into even smaller ones, I can easily eat it and enjoy it without harm." He takes a bite as Tim types.

"That's why, beneath those strategic objectives, you'll want to set goals and milestones," Barry says. "The key is to set goals and then break them down into milestones that you won't choke on instead of biting off more than you can chew. For example, let's say your strategic objective for the year is to grow your customer base. Your goal could be to get twenty customers that year. What do you think a good milestone would be?"

"You could aim for a certain number of paying customers in the next sixty days," Tim says.

"Great!" Barry exclaims. "You can then use the experiences from pursuing small goals to learn what works and what doesn't. But always keep in mind why you're doing it. Your purpose should always be your guiding light."

"How big are these goals and milestones?" Tim asks. "Months?"

"It varies," Barry says. "Goals usually match up with the strategic objectives. They should change every twelve to eighteen months or so as the business evolves. Milestones are smaller; they break up the process further. But remember, as you accomplish your goals, set new ones."

Tim nods, his fingers moving quickly over his keyboard.

"The main purpose of these smaller targets is to keep us focused on accomplishing tasks that align with our Three P's," Barry says. "And as the business evolves, whether we achieve our goals or not, we stay focused. If we don't meet our goals, we learn from the process; if we succeed, we move on to the next goal. It's about iteration and focus, not trying to do everything at once."

Tim glances at his notes.

Strategic Objectives

Level 1: 2–3 strategic objectives based on Three P's (12 months)

Level 2: 12-month goal(s)

Level 3: Milestones (variable/shorter)

"Now, as you work toward your strategic objectives, I've got a warning for you to keep in mind."

"Shoot," Tim says, picking up his drink.

"You have to avoid distractions," Barry says.

Tim laughs. His business is full of distractions.

"I know, I know," Barry says, holding up his hands. "I know you haven't set any strategic objectives just yet, but let me ask you this: How many of the activities you tackled at work last week aligned with your purpose?"

"Hmm," Tim says. "I think some of them did, yeah. Like the company-wide meeting I told you about. And the one-on-ones."

"That's excellent, Tim," Barry says, looking genuinely pleased. "I don't think you could have said that at the beginning of the year."

"Definitely not," Tim says with a laugh.

"It's great to see you growing like that," Barry says. "You've already started by building your foundation. And, once you formulate these strategic objectives, you have to remember to avoid distractions. Stay true to who you are and what you want to build. It's not about chasing every opportunity or every shiny object. It's about staying disciplined and saying no to the wrong things so you can say yes to the right ones."

"Got it," said Tim. "Don't bite off more than you can chew."

"Yep," Barry says, waving a chunk of walnut bar for emphasis. "We all see it with our clients—entrepreneurs getting distracted by new ventures or big customers that don't align with their original mission. You've got to keep your focus on building a business you love—one that makes money and adds value but also fulfills you. Do you remember my story about Matthew Emmons last week?"

"The Olympic shooter?" Tim says. "Yeah. I'm still cringing."

"I get it," Barry says, then pauses to down the rest of his coffee. "That's a great story about distractions and making sure you're aiming at the right targets. At the end of your life—because we're all going to die one day, hate to break the news—you'll ask yourself a lot of questions. Did you win? Did you lose? Did you hit the right target? Did what you did really matter? Will the people around you care? What would you do over if you could? What are your regrets? Will your legacy matter? These are all questions that can keep you focused on your vision in the long term."

Tim looks down, the weight of Barry's questions settling in. He would have so many regrets if his journey ended here and now. For years, he hadn't been living his life in a way that aligned with his purpose or created the impact he wanted to create. He had started to change that, but he had a long way to go.

"I encourage you to stay focused on what matters to you and prevent yourself from getting caught up in distractions," Barry says, seeming to read Tim's mind. "Be intentional about it today, because as you get older, that's what you'll want to be more and more focused on. Life flies by, and setting strategic objectives is one way to keep your business life in focus."

Tim nods. "You know, I didn't come to you with my personal life in mind, but I think this is the wake-up call I needed for that too."

"Better now than when it's too late," Barry says. "Glad to hear I've been of some use."

"That's an understatement. Thanks, Barry," Tim says, closing his laptop. "You've given me a lot to think about."

Barry smiles back and stands, hoisting his workout bag. "You're on the way to gold, Tim. Just keep aiming at the right target, and you'll get there."

Chapter 8 Summary

Scalable Business Framework: Strategic Objectives

Strategic Objectives
- Level 1: 2–3 strategic objectives based on the Three P's (12 months)
- Level 2: 12-month goal(s)
- Level 3: Milestones (variable/shorter)

Execution and Accountability
- Consistent methods of delivering results across the team.
- Regular check-ins and one-on-one meetings with employees.
- Feedback loops to refine and improve company processes.

Measuring Success and Improvement
- Structured scorecard for accountability and progress tracking.
- Client feedback collection and analysis.
- Net margin tracking.
- Operation refinement based on data and team insights.

Level 1-2-3 Strategic Objectives Worksheet

Prerequisites: Vision and Three P's

Vision:

To improve lives through excellence and service

Three P's

Purpose: *Peace*

People: *Serve*

Profit: *One*

Level 1: Strategic Objectives for 2025

Can we build a culture of trust with clients and employees?

Level 2: 12-Month Goal(s)

- Align internally with our vision.

- Develop consistency in our external results.

Level 3: Milestones (Variable Timing)

Establish the Vision:

- Conduct regular one-on-ones with each employee over the course of one month. — IN PROGRESS

- Develop a scorecard and questionnaire to guide the conversation and develop accountability by the end of the first quarter.

- Conduct a company training session on each of the Three Ps by the second quarter.

Focus on People (Team/Clients):

- Determine if the right people are in the right seats by the end of the second quarter. — IN PROGRESS

- Work with the team to identify the right type of client by the end of the year.

Measure Outcomes:

- Create a process to collect client feedback on each job and report it to the team overall and by employee.

- Build a method to capture net margin on a job level by the end of the third quarter.

- Develop a method all employees can use to get consistent results by the end of the year.

Learn more about strategic objectives and download a blank, printable version of this worksheet at ScalableBusinessFramework.com.

Chapter 9

Systems and Processes

Tim collapses into his usual chair across from Barry. He takes off his suit coat, which is spattered with rain, and uses it to mop his soaking face and hair.

"Why are you so dry?" he says grumpily.

"Hello to you, too," Barry says, smiling good-naturedly as he points to a black umbrella leaning on the window. "I got you your usual. And I snagged a little cheese board for us today."

"Thanks," Tim says, turning and throwing his sopping suit coat over the back of his chair. Outside, the world is a blur of gray water and dashing figures. Inside, the smell of fresh coffee lingers in the air, mingling with the faint warm smells of baked goods.

Tim absently sips his macchiato as Barry leans back, glancing out at the gray sky, then back at Tim.

"Sorry for the grumpy start. How are you today?" Tim says, feeling slightly better now that he's had a few sips of hot coffee. He pulls out his laptop, which has been mercifully protected by layers of fabric, from his bag.

"I'm splendid," Barry says. "Marathon training is going great. In fact, I'll be out of town next week during our usual time."

"*Another* marathon?" Tim asks, aghast.

"*Another* marathon," Barry replies, delighted. "This one's in California."

"Way to put the rest of us to shame," Tim says.

"Hey, it's not a competition," Barry says. "Would you like to meet online again?"

"Can do," Tim says, pulling out his strategic objectives worksheet and placing it on the table between them.

"Oh, yes, great," Barry says, peering at Tim's scrawl. "Okay, so your strategic objective is, 'Can we build a culture of trust with clients and employees?' That's very nice."

"Thanks," Tim says. "I thought it tied in well with our vision and Three P's, and it also addresses this serious culture shift we need to make. Which, after that meeting last week, already seems to be taking hold."

Barry looks curiously at Tim. "How so?"

"Well, people just seem happier around the office, for one," Tim says. "And a few days ago, a new client left a really nice review for us online saying our tech made them feel very comfortable during their initial visit. We haven't even done the work yet! Usually, we just get complaints about the on-site visit." He laughs.

"Excellent," Barry says. "I guess they were ready for change after all."

"It seems so," Tim says. "Okay, so back to the strategic objectives worksheet. I broke it down into two main goals. First, align internally on the vision, and second, develop consistency in our results. That addresses the team, the culture, and the service we offer our customers."

Barry taps his fingers lightly on the table. "You're right about that. And these milestones look really good as well. I like that you've divided them into three main categories here. What made you decide to do that?"

"Well," Tim says, "I thought it was important to establish the vision internally first, then get everyone—team and clients—on board. Then, finally, I put in some milestones for improving our processes for serving our clients and collecting feedback."

Barry leans back, nodding. "You've got a solid plan here, Tim. What's your biggest concern about following through?"

Tim exhales. "Honestly? Staying focused and not letting day-to-day distractions pull me away from these priorities. I know these objectives are critical, but it's easy to get caught up in the grind."

Barry nods, his expression serious. "That's a common challenge, but since you've spent a lot of time developing your vision and Three P's and you've chosen a strategic objective that aligns with them, it might actually be easier than you think."

Tim smiles, feeling encouraged. "Thanks, Barry. I'm ready to get moving on this."

Barry raises his coffee in a mock toast. "To the next twelve months of PEACE, SERVICE, and focusing on ONE job at a time. Now, let's talk about how you can achieve these objectives. It's time to talk about the Scalable Business Framework."

"Sounds important," Tim says, starting a new heading. He feels a strange sense of anticipation.

"It's incredibly important," Barry says. "The Scalable Business Framework is all about making your objectives attainable without driving you nuts."

"I can get behind that," Tim says, helping himself to a cracker and a piece of cheese from the cheese board, then adding a touch of jam to the top. "What kind of jam is this?"

"I don't know," Barry says. "You'll have to tell me."

Tim takes a bite and moans blissfully. "Fig," he says. "It's great with the Brie."

"Fig, Brie, and a good, solid cracker are a great combination," Barry says, smiling. "It reminds me a bit of the Three P's. They're like a triangle's three points. You can't have one without the others, and they all feed into each other and strengthen the other P's. The Scalable Business Framework works similarly, except instead of the Three P's, we have three new concepts: processes, automation, and visibility."

"Processes, automation, visibility," Tim mutters as he types.

"Just like we did with the Three P's, we'll go through those one at a time in great detail," Barry says, spreading fig jam on a cracker. "But first, let me explain the system and how it works. There are several key advantages I'd like to outline for you. First, there's a streamlined and stronger structure. I've got a question for you: If Google Sheets or Excel blew up tonight, what would you lose?"

Tim chuckles. "Probably a lot."

"For some businesses, it would be *everything*," Barry says, placing a slice of Brie onto his cracker. "Most small businesses start strong, doing what they're good at, but they hit a ceiling. That's when they start exhibiting something I call the MacGyver Syndrome."

"MacGyver?" Tim quirks an eyebrow. "The guy who could fix anything with a paperclip?"

"Yep, him," Barry says. "MacGyver would find himself in impossible situations and engineer solutions with whatever was lying around. It's impressive, but it's also reactive, and that's what a lot of businesses end up doing. They patch things together as they grow—new tools here, new processes there—just to keep things going."

Tim watches a couple dart across the street outside, umbrellas barely covering them. "That sounds a little too familiar."

"Hey, it's starting to change," Barry says. "And we're building processes all the time. Think about it—whether it's steps in your sales process, the way you onboard a client, or your service delivery method, it's all a series of steps designed to achieve a goal. The way these are implemented into an organization matters, though. Many business leaders do this with a focus on the immediate and urgent and not on the long term. The result over time is a mess. Eventually, a business might have nine or ten different tools and systems running their operations. One for sales, one for invoicing, one for lead generation, and probably a massive spreadsheet tracking all their deals. They built all of this to solve immediate problems, but not with intentionality. And definitely not with their Three P's in mind."

Tim grimaces. His deals *are* all on a spreadsheet.

"A whole business might be running on those Mac-Gyvered sheets or a tool that doesn't create scalability, and that's risky," Barry says, leaning forward to pick a few almonds off the cheese board. "It creates inefficiencies, bottlenecks, and chaos. People end up spending more time managing tools and processes than growing their business. The processes might not truly enforce their desired outcomes and who they want to be as a business.

"And that's where this framework steps in," he continues. "The Scalable Business Framework, SBF for short, helps mitigate that with better, intentional processes and tools that don't leave you vulnerable to a simple system failure."

"Like a shift to proactivity from reactivity," Tim says thoughtfully.

"Well said," Barry replies. "Business leaders respond to urgent stimuli and force a quick decision. If we can use the SBF to step back and think proactively, we can intentionally build a scalable system for growth."

Tim looks up from writing this down to find Barry munching his almonds and staring out the window, where the rain still lazily falls.

"That sounds really good so far," Tim says. "What's the next advantage?"

"Mental energy savings," Barry says. "How much mental energy do you think business owners spend thinking about their businesses when they're off the clock?"

Tim snorts. "A lot."

"That's the answer I get most often when I ask business leaders that question," Barry says, nodding. "It's always 'a lot.' And that's the thing—you're not just working in the business but also *outside* the business. You're mentally consumed by it even when you're not at the office."

"Mm-hmm," Tim says, taking a few almonds himself. He's delighted to find them warm.

"The Scalable Business Framework is great for reducing your mental load and creating systems that ensure your business can keep running regardless of the tools or the person in charge at any given moment," Barry explains. "The framework helps businesses put the right systems in place. You create streamlined processes, automate the tasks that shouldn't be sucking up your time, and get the visibility to actually see where things are going wrong. That's how you can build and scale without sacrificing your sanity. It becomes your engine for driving any objective and goal."

"Sounds a lot better than the status quo," Tim says. "Not to mention more efficient."

"You've already built a successful business; now you just need to run it and eventually scale it without letting it kill you," Barry says. "The Scalable Business Framework gives you mental space to focus on growth instead of just survival. You'll get the breathing room you need, not to just keep grinding away but to really thrive. You can move from working *in* the business to working *on* the business. The best news is that you'll no longer be the bottleneck on the business's growth."

Tim lets out a low whistle. "And you're saying this goes beyond just business impact, right? This has a personal impact, too?"

Barry smiles. "Absolutely. This is not just about making more money. It's about freeing up time and mental energy for the business owner. It's about getting back to being yourself—not being consumed by the business. As business owners, we know there's no such thing as work-life balance. That's a misnomer. Balance implies opposing forces. Your business—this entity that embodies your passion—shouldn't be working in opposition to your life. Developing a scalable and sustainable business using the SBF moves you closer to work-life integration."

Tim looks thoughtful as he watches the drizzle outside. "So, you're really talking about making a deeper, more meaningful change. Not just being more efficient. I can see how that connects really well with your emphasis on the work-life relationship."

Barry nods. "Exactly. We're helping people build businesses that are not just profitable but sustainable—businesses that allow them to live their lives again. Tim, to grow FastTrack, you and your leadership will have to pour into your team, who will pour into your customers. You can't ask anyone to pour from an empty cup."

Tim's fingers tap lightly on the table as he considers this. The smell of fresh pastries drifts from the counter, and the buzz of conversation surrounds them, but Tim's focus remains on the conversation. "That's a big deal. Huge, actually."

"Right," Barry says. "Now, on to the next advantage—return on luck."

Tim frowns. "Return on luck?"

"Return on luck," Barry says. "It's about being ready for opportunities when they come. Are you set up to capitalize on a sudden success, or would it crush you? If the number of clients you had multiplied by ten overnight, could you handle it? That's the real test. The Scalable Business Framework isn't just for handling day-to-day operations—it's for making sure you can scale when the time comes. It's about being ready for those moments of luck. Businesses that build for this capitalize on these moments."

Tim types the idea into his notes. "That's something I hadn't really thought about. But it makes sense."

Barry leans back. "It's all part of the bigger picture. The framework isn't just about solving today's problems—it's about building something that will last and meet all your business's needs."

Tim looks up, meeting Barry's eyes. "I'm starting to see how this all fits together. It's more than just fixing what's broken. You have to set the stage for something bigger."

"Exactly," Barry says, smiling as he takes a few grapes from the charcuterie board. "Speaking of which, let's discuss the next advantage: scalability. Growing a business isn't easy!"

"Tell me about it," Tim says, spreading jam on another cracker.

"If there were a simple trick or 'one cool thing to do to achieve growth,' people wouldn't struggle with it," Barry says. "It's simply a challenging process. Often leaders feel like they're doing all the right things, but there are factors beyond their control—things that seem to slip out of their grasp and hold them back."

"Yep," Tim says, taking a slice of cheese and placing it on his cracker.

"Here's what I've learned after working with hundreds of business leaders," Barry says. "Scaling doesn't happen by accident. Whether you're a start-up or a publicly traded company, the challenge remains the same. You need the proper strategy. And, most importantly, you need to execute it. That's another thing the Scalable Business Framework does. Your business will grow until you hit obstacles, even if you have the Three P's aligned. The SBF bypasses those walls and creates a business that doesn't rely on luck or heroics. It's about scaling smoothly, with structure."

"When I'm ready to try scaling again," Tim says, "that's how I want to do it."

"And I'm sure it'll go much better than the first time," Barry says. "Okay, now for the last advantage I want to discuss today. Like the Three P's, the SBF is an iterative system. You define your processes, automate what you can, and then get the visibility you need to track results. Every time you learn something, you adjust and improve. *That's how you scale.*"

"Like that flywheel you mentioned last week," Tim says. "Jim Collins?"

"I thought you said you had a bad memory." Barry's forehead wrinkles as he raises his eyebrows. "Exactly like that."

"So, the core principles of the SBF—process, automation, and visibility—are all interconnected," Tim says slowly, grabbing a few more almonds. "The key to making it scalable is its iterative nature."

"Right!" Barry says. "You learn why you win or lose, and adjust accordingly."

Tim's fingers hover over his keyboard for a moment as he absorbs this, then he types quickly, glancing back up. "So, it's like a feedback loop?"

"Exactly," Barry says, smiling. "It's a continuous loop of learning and improving. You don't just set up the processes once and forget about them. You're constantly revisiting them—refining, tweaking, optimizing. That's what makes the framework scalable. You're always learning from the data and iterating on the processes."

Tim looks out the window, watching the rain slide down the glass. A couple huddles under a small awning outside, waiting for the rain to stop. "That sounds like a really smart and dynamic way of running things."

"I love it," Barry says. "At Charis Strategies, we've built everything around this iterative approach. We automate wherever we can, but we also track results both internally and externally. That visibility into the data is what lets us make informed decisions. We check the results of our processes to see what's working and where things need to improve. Then we make adjustments."

He leans forward, his eyes alight. "That's how you scale. It's not a one-and-done kind of thing. It's a constant cycle of refining and improving."

Tim taps a few more notes into his laptop. "I like that. It's not about perfection on the first try—it's about making things better with each iteration."

Barry nods, setting his cup down with a soft clink. "Right. And with each iteration, you're not only improving the efficiency of your business but also freeing up more time and mental energy for you and your team to focus on bigger-picture things."

Tim rests his chin on his hand, absorbing this, looking over his notes.

Advantages of the Scalable Business Framework
- Stronger, streamlined structure
- Mental energy savings
- Return on luck
- Scalability
- Iterative nature (constant improvement)

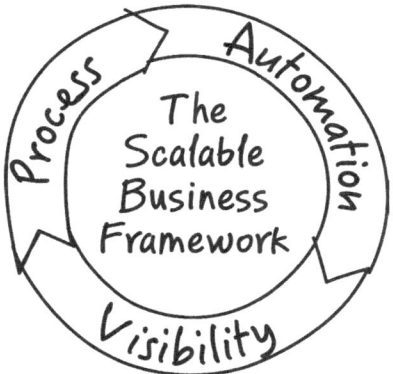

"Instead of setting things up once and walking away," he says, "you keep improving and adapting the whole thing as your business evolves."

"You bet," Barry says, picking up another cracker. The door to La Chance opens as a large group of twenty-somethings in trendy clothes exits. "It's about constant improvement. The system keeps refining itself. Think of it like a three-legged stool. If you're missing process, automation, or visibility, the whole thing wobbles. You can't scale if one of those legs is short." He nibbles a corner of the cheese, smiles, then puts the piece in his mouth.

"A three-legged stool, huh?" Tim says.

"Can you come up with a better analogy?" Barry says, smiling.

Tim hums, thinking, then says, "A human body without structure."

"That sounds like a trip to the ER," Barry quips.

Tim laughs. "Hear me out," he says. "Your processes are the musculoskeletal system—your bones and muscles. Without them, your business can't move, just like you couldn't get to the coffee shop if you didn't have your legs. You'd be like an amoeba."

Barry shakes his head, amused. "Okay, that's a picture I didn't need, but yes, that does work. Processes are the structure."

Barry layers a piece of cheese on his cracker, then says, "Actually, that analogy works on several levels. Take automation. That's like your autonomic nervous system—the stuff that runs on autopilot. Think about your breathing, your heartbeat. If you had to manually think about keeping your heart pumping while trying to have this conversation, you wouldn't get anything done. Businesses are the same. You've got to automate the essential functions so your people can focus on higher-order tasks."

Tim leans back in his chair, crossing his arms. This hits home for him. "I've been running around manually pumping that heart and digesting food and all that other stuff," he says, making a face. "Yeah, I guess a lot of our team spends time on things we could probably automate."

Barry nods. "That's where we see businesses falter. They're so busy manually managing basic tasks that they can't take on bigger, more strategic work. Once you automate those processes, it frees up your team to focus on what really matters."

Tim raises his hand as if signaling. "Okay, so we've got the structure and automation. What about visibility?"

Barry points to the cup in front of him, from which steam still drifted upward, then looks back at Tim. "Visibility is like your sensory system—sight, hearing, touch. It lets you perceive what's happening around you and react accordingly. In business, that's your data. You need a clear view of your operations to see where things are working and where they're falling short. It's like knowing when to stop drinking a scalding cup of coffee, or to pull your hand away from a hot stove."

Tim chuckles. "You've really hijacked my analogy. So, if I don't have visibility, I'll just keep burning myself?"

Barry nods, gesticulating with his cheese and cracker. "Exactly. That's why you need to track results and adjust. Charis Strategies works with businesses that rely on massive spreadsheets to track deals, like I said, but that system doesn't give them the insight they need to see the whole picture."

"I feel judged," Tim says, pulling a face.

"Hey, not all spreadsheets are bad," Barry says with a laugh. "They're great for piloting a process or for ad hoc analysis. With some automation and the right reports and data, you get that clarity—both internally and externally—so you can make smarter decisions and scale." He finally eats the piece of cracker he's been waving around.

Tim takes a grape, savoring its juicy tang as he looks out the window into the rain. "It makes sense," he says finally. "I've definitely been flying blind in some areas, and my team's stuck in the same cycle. I guess it's like trying to run a race with no legs, no breathing, and no idea where the finish line is. Bad idea."

Barry grins, leaning back in his chair. "That's a pretty good analogy too! You're on a roll today. Anyway, once you've got those three principles in place—processes, automation, and visibility—it all starts to click. It's not about adding more tools; it's about making everything work together in a scalable way."

Tim nods, starting to see the bigger picture. He types some more notes, the gears in his head already turning. "I can see how that would make a difference. So, the whole framework really boils down to balancing those three?"

Barry picks up his cup, smiling. "Exactly. Let's go back to the stool analogy. If one of those three legs is short, the whole thing falls. But when they're all working together, your business can scale smoothly. And the best part? You're always learning and improving. It's a continuous loop."

"Okay," Tim says. "I'm excited about this. I can see how it will make a big difference for my business."

"Great!" Barry says. "That's the quick and dirty introduction. Before we talk about what you need to do next, let's take a second to acknowledge what you've already done. Before we even get into the framework, there are some prerequisites you need in place."

"The Three P's?" Tim guesses.

"Yes!" Barry says, throwing up his hands just as a bright bolt of lightning strikes in the distance. Barry and Tim sit, blinking, for a second.

"Well, that was more dramatic than I anticipated," he says. Both men start laughing, and for a couple of minutes, nothing productive happens at their table.

"Okay, okay, the Three P's," Barry says, still chuckling. "First and foremost, you need a vision—a purpose, like the one you identified after our first meeting. This is well summarized in Jim Collins and Jerry Porras's book *Built to Last*.[34] Basically, vision is about more than just where you want to go in the short term. It includes your values, your purpose, and your big, hairy, audacious goal."

Leaning forward, Barry rests his chin in his interlaced fingers, propping his elbows on the table. "The BHAG is your moonshot," he says, "but vision also includes values—those timeless, enduring principles that guide everything you do—and purpose, which is your 'why.' For some people, finding their why can be as sudden and dramatic as that bolt of lightning a few minutes ago. But for others, it can take some time to really sort through what values should guide

---

34 Collins and Porras, *Built to Last*, 94–98.

you, and that's okay. No matter how you get there, if you can find your why, you'll find your way."

Tim nods slowly, absorbing this. Outside, a man with an enormous red umbrella strolls by, pausing to glance into the shop before moving on.

Barry continues. "And having the right team in place is just as critical. Even with the best processes, if your team isn't aligned with your vision and purpose, it's going to be an uphill battle. Your people need to buy into your values and your mission if they're going to help you scale."

Tim leans back in his chair, his fingers drumming lightly on the table. "That makes sense. If the team isn't on board, everything else starts to fall apart. Good thing my team likes me a little better these days."

"Definitely," Barry agrees, "because this is going to be hard work. Making this transition is painful! It's completely worth it, but your company's culture was built one way, and now you're moving to a more professionalized, disciplined culture."

"Right," Tim says. "At least in my case, I've already started improving the culture, and everyone seems pretty happy about it overall. Maybe that will make them more receptive to further changes."

"I think so," Barry says. "It's only once you've got that purpose and the right team, and you know what strategic objectives will help you be profitable, that you can start thinking about the framework itself. It's not just something random—this never would have worked if we'd started with the framework without discussing the P's first. So, basically, give yourself a big pat on the back."

Tim does so, grinning. Barry chuckles.

"Now we're going to narrow down and start on systems and processes."

Tim types a new heading on his screen. "Quick question," he says, looking at this heading. "I thought the SBF term was *processes*. Why *systems* too? Is it just because of the acronym?"

"Very perceptive," Barry says. "Systems are collections of processes. You have to build the individual processes to make a system."

"Oh, okay," Tim says.

"Now let's revisit your human body analogy from earlier," Barry says. "In that analogy, processes are the musculoskeletal system of your business. The musculoskeletal system—your set of muscles, tendons, and bones—enables movement. Without it, you'd be, well, kind of like an amoeba, like you said. You wouldn't be able to go to the store, go to work, or really do anything."

Tim chuckles. "Yeah, I'd rather not be an amoeba."

Barry grins back at him. "It's the same thing with your business. Without solid processes, your business can't function, much less grow and scale. Processes keep everything moving. They're the bones and muscles of your operation."

Tim nods, glancing out the window where a few pedestrians are strolling past, umbrellas tucked away now as the rain ebbs. "Okay, that makes sense. So, processes are like the backbone of the business."

"Right," Barry says. "There are four key advantages of processes and systems I'd like to highlight for you. First, processes provide consistency. When you don't execute consistently, you get a lot of variance in how things are done, and that makes it almost impossible to repeat results.

"Let's say one day you want to exit your business. A potential buyer looks at how repeatable your results are. They want their investment to pay off into the future. If everything depends on internal knowledge—stuff that only certain people know—that's not attractive to a buyer."

Tim nods, grabbing his mug. "Yeah, I guess if the business can't run without key people, it's not really scalable."

"Exactly," Barry says. "What you need to do is take all that internal knowledge, work with your team, and build it into a system. Once it's documented and everyone follows it, you get repeatable results. That's the foundation of a scalable business."

Tim mulls this over. "So, it's about more than just creating order—it's about making sure things can run without being dependent on any one person."

"Right," Barry continues. "It's also kind to your employees. The people doing the day-to-day work need processes and systems that are easy to use. They need processes that are simple and consistent so everyone's on the same page. If your team isn't aligned, you're going to run into trouble. Consistency keeps things clean and accurate."

"And here's the thing: consistency compounds," Barry says. "The more your team works with the same process, the better they get at it. Over time, they're iterating and improving, getting 1 percent better every day. That's how you build something scalable. Once you focus on consistency, finding something that isn't working becomes much easier as well. You have more data to judge if a portion of a process is accomplishing the goal."

Tim nods. "Iterative. Like the SBF as a whole."

"Right," Barry says, stacking a cracker and a piece of cheese. "And that brings us to the next point—clarity. Processes create clarity for your team. When everyone knows exactly what to do and how to do it, they don't have to figure things out on their own. It's a breath of fresh air.

"Like consistency, clarity is kindness," Barry says, holding his cracker and cheese stack between two fingers. "When you give your team clear, prescriptive steps, you're setting them up for success. A lot of businesses don't have well-defined processes because they fear being too rigid, but having a defined process actually creates freedom for their team. It gives them a clear path to follow, which results in more consistent outcomes."

Tim leans back in his chair. "That makes sense. When people know what's expected, it takes a lot of pressure off them and makes everything easier."

Barry nods. "It's also good for business. That's the third advantage—systems and processes create a baseline for success. When your team has clear processes to follow, they're going to be successful 80–85 percent of the time. For the other 15 percent, they can ask for help. But the point is you've established a baseline for success. You can hand something to your team and say, 'If you follow this process, it will work most of the time.' That creates confidence and helps eliminate a lot of the guesswork. You can then manage the exceptions and improve the process long term."

"Okay," Tim says, his voice more thoughtful now. "So, processes create consistency, they give your team clarity, and they establish a baseline for success. I can see how that would help make things run smoother."

Barry smiles, leaning back in his chair. "And there's one more key thing—scalability, just like with the SBF as a whole. A business can't scale without well-defined processes. When you're small, it's easy to patch things together and make 'em work, but if you want to grow, your processes need to grow with you. They're the foundation that your business can stack more volume on without breaking down."

Tim taps his fingers lightly on the table, his mind turning over the information. "So, without systems and processes, scaling isn't even an option."

"Exactly," Barry says, leaning forward again. "Systems and processes are the cornerstone of effective scaling, and that's where leaders often get stuck. When we talk about processes, we're addressing one of the biggest barriers businesses face when trying to scale. At this point, Charis Strategies has worked with nearly a thousand clients and completed over two thousand projects. What you're hearing today is distilled from all that experience—mistakes, wins, everything."

Tim looks over his notes as Barry polishes off a few more almonds.

Advantages of Systems and Processes
1. Consistency
2. Clarity
3. Baseline for Success
4. Scalability

"I want in," he says. "How do I create these processes?"

"Let's get into the key elements of a good process," Barry suggests. "We've talked about why processes are important, but what actually makes a process effective?"

Tim glances down at his laptop, fingers poised over the keys. "Yeah, that's the part I'm curious about. How do you make sure a process actually works?"

"Well," Barry begins, grabbing his mug, "it's time for another list."

Tim starts a new list: Components of Effective Processes.

"It all starts with defining the **right** path," Barry says. "You need to think about the end goal—what's the best possible outcome? Once you know that, you backtrack and plan out how to get there. What's the ideal way to reach your goal?"

Tim nods, typing. "So, start with the end in mind and work backward."

"Exactly," Barry says. "And once you've figured out that right path, you need to break it down into descriptive steps. You can't be vague here—each step needs clear entry and exit criteria. That way, your team knows when one step is done and when to move on to the next."

Tim pauses, his brow furrowed in thought. "Entry and exit criteria?"

"The pieces of data required to move from one step to the next in the process," Barry explains. "The process should be built in a way that prevents the team from moving from step to step without these critical pieces of information. We'll talk more about that next week."

"Okay," Tim says.

"But here's the thing," Barry continues enthusiastically. "Defining steps in the process isn't enough. You also need to define right behaviors along the way."

Tim leans back. "What does that mean?"

"A lot of folks design processes with a 'data requirements and steps only' approach, but that's only half the battle," Barry explains, taking a few more grapes. "I always encourage folks to take a step back and think about what behaviors and communications will guarantee success here. Those aren't data points, but they're steps toward success.

"Let's use the sales process as an example. Sure, the main steps might be something like a discovery call, a proposal, showing the proposal, and closing the deal. But what else should your team be doing at each stage?"

Tim nods slowly. "Like follow-ups or specific emails?"

"Yes," Barry says, smiling. "At Charis Strategies, for instance, our team started reaching out two or three weeks into a project to ask, 'How's the project going? Is everything meeting your expectations?' That made a huge difference. That little check-in helped us identify any issues early, close expectation gaps, and improve client satisfaction. So, we made that behavior part of our process."

"That's smart," Tim says, typing away. "I can do that."

"And then there's the question of right data," Barry says. "Every process needs certain data points to run smoothly downstream. This is especially important when it comes to reporting. If you don't have the right data, you can't measure success. Good data requirements help keep your team on the right track *and* give you the ability to evaluate the process later."

Tim's fingers pause over the keyboard. "So, you build the process in a way that forces people to capture the right data?"

"Exactly," Barry says. "But we won't worry about that until next week, either. For now, your homework is simply to define three key processes that would make the biggest difference for your company that include the right path (with descriptive steps), the right behaviors, and the right data."

"Okay," Tim says. "I have some ideas already." He looks at his notes.

Components of Effective Processes
1. Right path
2. Right behaviors
3. Right data

"Be sure to get your team's input on these and ensure everyone is on the same page," Barry instructs. "You may discover the process wasn't as clear as you thought. Leaders can't let this type of objective be just top-down. You need bottom-up buy-in so your team will have ownership in the process and the process will be more detailed and accurate."

"Right, for sure," Tim says, writing this down. Outside, the sidewalk is dotted with puddles. The coffee shop is packed now with people who came in to get out of the rain.

Tim takes a deep breath, setting his laptop aside. "All right, I'm going to give this some real thought. Thanks for today."

Barry smiles, stacking their empty mugs atop the demolished cheese board. "It's a lot to digest, I know. But once you start breaking it down, you won't believe the difference it makes. A good process isn't just about getting things done—it lets you build something that works consistently, scales with your business, and ultimately drives success."

"And here's one final tip. You know what the right process is? It's the one that works! Don't overanalyze and try to get things perfect. Put the best process in place based on the information you have, measure the outcomes, and iterate as necessary. The key is to get started and stay consistent."

"That sounds good to me," Tim says, grinning. "Looking forward to talking next week, Barry. And, hey—good luck with that marathon."

Chapter 9 Summary

Scalable Business Framework: Systems and Processes

Advantages of the Scalable Business Framework
- Stronger, streamlined structure
- Mental energy savings
- Return on luck
- Scalability
- Iterative nature (constant improvement)

Advantages of Systems and Processes
- Consistency
- Clarity
- Baseline for success
- Scalability

Components of Effective Processes
- Right path
- Right behaviors
- Right data

Learn more about systems and processes and download a comprehensive process design guide at ScalableBusinessFramework.com.

Chapter 10

Processes and CRMs

Tim adjusts his earbuds, leaning back in his office chair as the video call connects.

"Hi, Tim!" Barry says enthusiastically. He appears to be sitting outside, the California sun casting a warm glow behind him. Tim glances at the cityscape beyond his own windows; a light drizzle taps against the glass. How depressing.

"Looks like you've been enjoying yourself," Tim says, glancing at the vista behind Barry.

Barry chuckles, lifting a glass of red wine. "Yeah, just wrapped up the Napa Valley Marathon a couple of days ago. Stuck around for a little wine and downtime with my wife. But don't worry, I'm still ready to talk business."

"Congrats on the marathon," Tim replies, lifting his coffee mug. It's still full of drip coffee, but since he started buying better beans and invested in a new coffee machine with a built-in grinder for the office, it isn't nearly as bad as it was. "How are you feeling?"

"Sore," Barry admits.

"I can only imagine," Tim says. "I don't think I have any marathons in my future."

"You never know," Barry says, his eyes alight. "How's the family?"

"The baseball league has their first game this coming weekend," Tim says. "I'm actually going to be there. For real."

"I believe you." Barry takes a sip of his wine and leans forward. "All right, let's dive in. Which areas did you identify that need new or improved systems and processes?"

"The first thing I thought of was my sales process," Tim says, opening his notes doc. "My team is already doing on-site visits and proposals, but we don't have clear entry and exit criteria for each step. They don't know exactly what data to gather at each stage. We're getting inconsistent results from the team, and it impacts how we can perform for clients."

"That sounds right," Barry says. "A lack of clarity as to what data to gather is actually one of the biggest system-related problems that keeps businesses from growing."

"Really?" Tim asks.

"You bet," Barry says, leaning back in his chair. "Without the right data, you can't learn and update your processes. You repeat the same mistakes and won't scale."

"Makes sense," Tim says.

"This happens across organizations," Barry says, "but I pick on sales because all businesses have that motion. There are two primary data issues in sales processes. The first is what I call pipeline ignorance—leaders not knowing what's in their sales pipeline. This happens when sales teams operate without a standardized process. Salespeople gather varying degrees of data. Some don't track sales efforts, and some do. They aren't accountable to a single, defined process to accomplish their mission. You don't really have a clear idea of what's going on, and therefore you can't coach your team effectively."

"Okay, well, I hope my plan for today covers that," Tim says. "What about the second?"

"Lagging pipeline," Barry says. "This is when the sales process isn't being updated in real time. Information is updated sparingly and at different points depending on the salesperson. Much of the time, leaders only see new deals and won deals; everything else is unmanaged. Information is updated only when the leader forces a sales meeting. At that point, it's too late to manage or coach."

Tim nods again. "Yeah, that definitely happens."

"The solution is to standardize the process so that everyone is working from the same playbook. Once you get the sales process standardized, like we'll talk about today," Barry says, "it fixes those issues. You can start building out the rest of the system. But I'm getting ahead of myself.

Could you walk me through the steps you identified for your sales process?"

"Yeah, sure," Tim says. "I've put together a document showing our process and some of the potential areas for improvement I've identified. Here, let me share it with you."

"Got it," Barry says, clicking. Tim pulls the document up on his second monitor. Barry leans closer to the camera, eyes narrowing as he reviews the details while Tim begins to explain.

"So, this is basically how our sales process works at the moment," Tim says. "It's a five-step process. We start with an initial call to see what the customer needs."

"That sounds pretty standard," Barry says. "What's going wrong at this stage?"

"Actually, not a lot," Tim says. "Just identifying our vision and Three P's went a long way toward helping us tweak this first step. Do you remember when I made that list of questions to get to the 'why' for each customer?"

"I do," Barry says. "You told me that it helped you realize that one customer had a child with asthma, isn't that right?"

"Yeah," Tim says. "And it's been working just as well since. It helps us dig beyond basic facts and get to motivations, constraints, and client expectations so we fulfill our purpose."

Barry smiles. "Good. You want your team to listen actively and adapt based on the client's responses."

"I actually think that's the ideal behavior part we talked about last week," Tim says. "We were already moving toward that without actually knowing the terminology, and we're therefore already seeing results and better customer satisfaction."

"Exactly," Barry agrees. "And once you've laid that groundwork, it's time to document those behaviors and criteria in a way that leaves no room for ambiguity. How are you documenting them at the moment?"

"Ah," Tim says. "Well, I'm just having the sales reps leave a little note in the CRM. We had the meeting, so I guess I just expected them to go do it from now on."

"That's not bad," Barry says, "but today you'll learn how to improve on it. For instance, at Charis Strategies, we found that outlining behavioral expectations—like always summarizing a call in an email recap—helped the team maintain consistency and accountability. We do this in our CRM so every time someone works a new deal, they clearly see the expectations and can execute them."

Tim nods, typing this into his notes. "A summary email to the client—simple but effective. I hadn't thought of that. That could bridge a lot of our current gaps."

"It's small things like that," Barry says. "Those actions reinforce reliability and transparency, which clients appreciate."

"Okay, so next, there's the on-site visit," Tim says. "Customers sometimes complain afterward about having told the tech something that ended up being forgotten. They don't feel heard, and it creates mistakes and dissatisfaction."

Barry frowns slightly. "That's an engagement issue as well as a recordkeeping one. Capturing and remembering these less obvious details is essential. How can you adjust the team's process?"

"Well, obviously we need to get those customer-specific details," Tim says. "The initial call is broader, but during the on-site visit, we have to get much more technical so we can provide the quote. Again, that's something we've already made a lot of progress on."

"Do you have a list I could see?" Barry asks. Behind him, a few birds fly past.

"Sure," Tim says, sending it over. As Barry scans the list, Tim hears a tap on his door. It's Erica, one of his managers, holding a paper pastry bag and wearing a smile. Tim waves her in.

"I went to La Chance for coffee, and I got this for you," she whispers, sliding the bag onto Tim's desk.

"Erica, come say hi to Barry," Tim says warmly. "He's the consultant behind a lot of the changes we've been seeing around here."

Erica's face lights up. She walks around the desk and waves at Barry.

"Thank you so much for all the work you've been doing with Tim," she says enthusiastically. "I can't even explain how different things are around here now. I love the one-on-one meetings with my team, and Tim seems so much happier too."

"Glad to hear it, Erica," Barry says. "It's very nice to meet you."

Erica shows herself out after a few more pleasantries. Tim thanks her for the pastry and watches her leave, thinking, *She really used to hate me, and I don't blame her at all. What a change.*

"She seems very nice," Barry says.

"She's been thrilled with the changes," Tim says, peering into the bag. It's a spinach and feta pastry roll. His stomach rumbles as he pulls it out.

"Back to your list," Barry says, as Tim places the pastry on top of the bag. "I like that this goes deeper than the standard items like square footage, home construction type, and insulation. And I really like that you encourage the sales reps to reference the 'why' from the initial call. Knowing that can change exactly what you recommend for the client."

"Absolutely," Tim says. "And it also helps to know some of this other stuff. How do they schedule their thermostat? Are there aesthetic factors to consider? Any specialty needs like zones, UV lighting, or humidifiers? It all plays a role."

"Based on thinking about processes, what do you think you could tweak here?" Barry asks.

"Well, I was thinking we could have the techs repeat back what the client said at the end of each visit. Something like, 'Just to make sure we're aligned, here's what I heard you mention: You want to make sure the new system is energy-efficient because of budget concerns, and you'd like a solution that doesn't disrupt your nursery setup.' And then, of course, we make sure to record all that information properly."

Barry smiles. "Great! It's a simple step, but it reinforces that the client's voice is valued. It's also a good opportunity for the client to clarify or add any missed points."

"That will make a big difference," Tim agrees. "And it would help prevent those situations when a client says, 'I told you that the first time you were here.'"

"Yes," Barry says, leaning in. "And recording what you learn also builds trust. The whole team can access these critical details and emphasize them with the client later on, which helps clients feel heard. Clients who feel heard are more likely to feel confident in the service and more willing to collaborate openly. It turns the process from a transaction into a partnership. Plus, if you make that a consistent practice, it becomes part of your team's culture. Clients will know they're working with professionals who truly care about their specific needs, not just the technical details."

Tim nods. "I'll add that follow-up step and train the team to implement it during every on-site visit. This way, we don't just avoid mistakes—we build stronger relationships."

Tim and Barry spend more time combing through each step of his sales process, and Tim shares all his ideas, from making estimates and proposals faster and more scalable to standardizing follow-ups.

"The thing is," Tim says, scratching his head, "I know what to do now. I'm just not totally sure how to implement it. I know how you feel about spreadsheets . . ."

Barry lets out a hearty laugh, his wine glass glowing ruby red in the California sun. "Well," he says, grinning, "I think today's topic will take care of a lot of this for you, so don't look so glum. Today's main topic is balancing technology with good processes, and you're a step ahead because you already have a CRM. As soon as I mention CRMs to someone who doesn't have one, they immediately want to know about the numbers. What's the cost? What's the return on investment?"

"Good questions," Tim says. "Sometimes I wonder if it's worth it, honestly. It's pretty pricey." He takes another bite of the warm, flaky pastry.

"Well, I can give them plenty of statistics," Barry says, "like the fact that companies implementing CRMs often see up to a 100 percent increase in conversion rates. Or that for every dollar spent on a CRM, they get $8.71 back."[35]

Tim frowns slightly. "I don't think it's making that much of a difference for me."

"Well, it all depends on how the system is built and how you're using it," Barry says. "I'm sure you've talked to others who use CRMs. Some love their CRM, and others hate it, even if they have the same one."

"That's true," Tim says. "It's a polarizing topic."

---

[35] "CRM Pays Back $8.71 for Every Dollar Spent," Nucleus Research, June 2014, https://nucleusresearch.com/research/single/crm-pays-back-8-71-for-every-dollar-spent.

"That's because not everyone knows how to use them effectively," Barry explains. "The difference isn't so much the tool as the way it's implemented. Many CRMs have the same high-level features, but their users get wildly different results."

"There's nothing worse than being a business owner who feels trapped in a bad system. I never want my clients to think, *I have this technology platform and a successful business, but I can't scale because it won't do what I need.* As a business consultant, I treat my client's business like it's my own and guide them to make smart decisions, especially when it comes to flexibility. By treating our client's business as our own, we make sure they're getting the most out of their investment and they have the tools and flexibility to scale without feeling trapped. So usually, instead of focusing only on the immediate ROI, I start digging deeper. That's when we move from just talking about numbers to addressing the actual pain points."

"Pain points?" Tim asks.

"Yes," Barry says, the speaker crackling slightly in a light breeze. "Let's talk about latent versus active pain. Active pain is obvious. Clients come to us with Phase 1 problems—bottlenecks, inefficiencies, things they want fixed right away. That's the urgent stuff, like quadrant one in the time management matrix."

Tim frowns. "What?"

"The time management matrix, sometimes called the Eisenhower Matrix,"[36] Barry says. "There are four quadrants based on urgency and importance. Those Phase 1 problems are things that are important *and* urgent."

"Okay," Tim says, making himself a little chart in his notes.

"But then there's latent pain—the stuff business owners aren't fully aware of yet," Barry says. "That's where the real challenge lies. It's our job to surface that pain, to make them see the importance of tackling it before it becomes a real problem." Barry looks up for a moment, thinking, then his face lights up. "It's like someone who drinks a venti mocha from Starbucks every morning, gains fifteen pounds over five years, and doesn't realize each drink has 500 calories. They don't want to confront it, but that doesn't make the problem go away."

Tim chuckles, glancing at his coffee with a dash of milk—no sugar. He's now dropped fifteen pounds. "Yeah, I know what you mean. It's easy to ignore things when they don't seem urgent."

Barry nods. "That's why quadrant two—important but not urgent—is where you get the most value. When clients focus on those issues, they see the biggest long-term benefits. But first we have to help them realize the importance of addressing those latent pain points."

Tim looks over his notes.

---

36 Covey, *Seven Habits*.

Time Management Matrix

	Urgent	Not Urgent
Important	Urgent and important (crisis)	Not urgent but important (focus here)
Not Important	Urgent but not important (time waster)	Not urgent and not important (no value)

"So it's about getting ahead of the problems before they hit, right?" Tim asks.

"Exactly," Barry says, leaning forward and setting his glass down. The stem causes a blur on the side of the screen. "Focusing on the important and not urgent quadrant first reduces the urgent and important quadrant over time. Reducing the urgent and important quadrant items takes that constant state of emergency out of a business. It removes the chaos."

"I could use less chaos in my business," Tim says.

"We all could," Barry says, smiling. "It's also about discussing the opportunity cost. A lot of times, ROI statistics aren't enough to convince someone. So we ask, 'What are you giving up by not making this investment? What happens if you get ten times your revenue and lead flow tomorrow?

Could you manage it? Are your systems and processes in place to handle that kind of growth?'"

Tim sits up a little straighter, tapping a note into his laptop. "Right, like the 'return of luck' concept. If you don't have the right systems, a big win could quickly turn into a nightmare."

"Exactly," Barry says, nodding. "The point is, you have to *prepare* for growth. If a business isn't set up to scale, a sudden windfall could crush it. I often work with clients who use specialized systems tailored to their industry, but those often don't cut it. They don't integrate well with other parts of the business. They're often rigid, and if the provider goes out of business, you're stuck."

Tim nods. "I could see that. But, to be honest, I don't find my CRM all that great either."

"You will soon," Barry says. "The key is customizing your CRM to fit your business. The best CRMs are flexible platforms and more than just customer management tools. They can handle service, account management, some HR tasks, even parts of accounting and payments."

Tim's eyes widen slightly. "Well, I'm not using it like that."

"Technology is crucial, but it's not the magic fix," Barry says. "You can have the best tech in the world, but if you're not using it well, it won't matter. The other thing is that this won't work until you've identified good processes. If your processes are broken, it won't matter. You need good processes in place before the technology can help you scale. Think of it this way: Having your processes outlined on paper or in a spreadsheet won't drive effective growth by itself. That's why you did your homework."

"Yeah, I'm feeling good about what I've outlined," Tim says. "And I've already got a CRM. So now I just have to mash the two together."

"Right, so let's forge ahead," Barry says, scooting his glass a little to the side so it isn't blocking the camera. "CRMs work so well for building processes, in part because they allow you to enforce validation rules—basically, making sure the minimum data requirements are met before moving to the next step."

"Like what?" Tim asks, sitting back. Outside his window, a miserable-looking wet bird flies past.

"Well, for example, let's say you're moving from a discovery call to building a proposal," Barry says, his voice crackling slightly over the connection for a moment before stabilizing again. "Before you can start the proposal, you need to know the client's goal, their timeframe, and their budget. Those are the data requirements for that stage. And once you have those data checkpoints in place, you can start analyzing the process. Are there bottlenecks? Where is the process working well? Where are you losing deals, and why? By capturing and analyzing that data, you can identify areas to improve."

"Ohhhh," Tim says. "Yeah, I'm not doing anything like that in my CRM. Actually, could you hang on?"

"Sure," Barry says. Tim gets up for a moment and, leaving his office, walks out onto the floor. The hum of phone conversation continues around him, and a few people turn and smile at him as he walks over to a cubicle near the center of the room. He also passes quite a few empty cubicles; some of the staff are working from home today.

Finally, he reaches his destination: the cubicle of a slight woman in a green sweater.

"Hi, Wendy," Tim says. "How's your afternoon going?"

"It's going well," Wendy says, smiling up at him. "Can I help you with something?"

"Actually, if you have a minute, could you come with me?" Tim asks. "I'd like you to sit in on some of this meeting I'm having with my business consultant. He's talking about integrating processes into CRMs."

Wendy pops out of her chair, sliding a laptop off the desktop. "I'd love that," she says.

The two of them go back to Tim's office, and Tim slides a chair around the side so she can join him in front of the webcam.

"Barry, this is Wendy," Tim says. Wendy gives a small wave. "She's our CRM guru. Wendy, meet Barry, our amazing business consultant."

Barry grins back. "Nice to meet you, Wendy. Just the person to have in this meeting."

"Glad to be here," Wendy says. "Hey, the two of you are like two peas in a pod. Tim, is this a family member of yours?"

Tim laughs. "No, but it's starting to feel like it sometimes."

Barry chuckles and nods. "At Charis Strategies, we're one big family," he says.

"Barry," Tim asks, "could you repeat what you said a minute ago about data checkpoints?"

Barry does, and Wendy starts typing at lightning speed on her laptop.

"You also need to make sure your processes are customizable and scalable, like we discussed last week," Barry says. "CRMs are great because they can grow with you. You don't want something rigid that breaks as your business expands." He picks up something small from off camera and eats it.

"That's why a CRM can be so powerful to help grow and scale," he continues. "If your team can accomplish the goal without going through the process, you don't have a process. Good process requires accountability, which requires a method to hold the team accountable. If you don't have a strong process that promotes accountability, you can't scale effectively."

Tim nods. "Yes, that makes a lot of sense. And the data? How do you make sure it's all getting captured?"

Barry takes another sip of wine. "You set validation rules. Let's say, for example, that before your team can send out a proposal, they need to fill out certain fields about the client's goals and budget. If those fields aren't filled in, the system won't let them move on to the next step. They get an error until all required fields are filled. It keeps everyone accountable."

Tim smiles, feeling himself getting excited about the possibilities. "I like that idea."

"And once you have that," Barry says, "you can start tracking everything. You'll be able to see where your process is airtight and where it might be leaking. You can figure out why you're winning or losing deals and make adjustments accordingly."

"This is great stuff," Wendy says, her fingers flying across the keyboard. "I do have to ask, though—I can see this initially making things more difficult for the team as they navigate the learning curve. We might get some complaints about those error messages. Anything we can do about that?"

Barry nods. "In the long term, having this data prevents communication errors and delays internally and will help the team get better," he says. "You're right—many times, end users don't see it that way at first. They see more information to fill out and requirements to complete a job. But if we help people see the long-term benefits, involve them in the process design, and provide lots of support during the learning process, people eventually get on board. Over time, you'll build in some automation to make the whole process easier. Does that make sense?"

"Sure does," Wendy says.

"I'm glad you think so," Barry says. "Now, Wendy, I can put you in touch with my own CRM guru to help you get some of this set up later if you'd like."

"That would be lovely," she says, nodding enthusiastically.

"Great," Barry says, leaning back and looking up at the cerulean sky. "Now, let me give you an example of how this can work. I have a client called The Spice Mart that manufactures spices—custom blends that companies come to them for. Their old process included sending out samples to clients, but they weren't tracking them well. They'd send out samples, never hear back, and then lose track of the opportunities entirely. And if you don't follow up on those samples, you don't close the deal."

Tim frowns. "So, they had no way of knowing if the samples led to a sale?"

"Exactly," Barry says. "They were tracking everything in a spreadsheet, but it wasn't enough. It quickly became outdated and inaccurate."

"Those darn spreadsheets again," Tim says jokingly.

"Right, the MacGyvered spreadsheets," Barry says with a laugh. "Needless to say, they were missing out on qualified opportunities. So, we helped them by building a sample process into the existing sales process within their CRM. We created a custom object that sits below the opportunity."

Tim tilts his head. "A custom object? What's that?"

"In a CRM, an object is essentially a data structure," Wendy says, chiming in. "It's like a new tab on a spreadsheet.

It has a relationship to the other tabs, which can help with reporting and process organization. If you build a custom object specifically for sample tracking, you could integrate it directly into a sales process."

Barry taps his temple, smiling at Wendy. "Exactly right. We put in an object so that once a sales rep reaches a certain stage in the sales cycle, they're prompted to go through the sample process. This ensures the sales rep follows up and tracks each sample properly."

Tim leans back. "So, now they can track the samples and see if they lead to a closed deal?"

"Exactly," Barry says. "They can now report on every sample, build list views, and manage those opportunities better. The result? More consistent follow-through and ultimately more closed sales. It was a small change, but it had a huge impact."

Tim smiles. "That sounds like a game-changer."

Barry nods. "It really was. It's a perfect example of how building a process within a CRM platform can drastically improve the way a business operates. And the best part is, you don't need a dedicated tech team to manage it."

"I've got Wendy," Tim points out, and she smiles.

"That's true, and I'm sure she's fantastic at what she does," Barry says, nodding. "But she's just one person. These tools help you grow with the staff you already have without losing flexibility or being tied down to a provider that can't adapt to your needs. In other words, it's consistent, clear, and scalable, and it provides a baseline for success."

"Okay, got it," Tim says. "I think I can guess what my homework is for next week." Barry gives Tim a questioning look.

"Wendy and I have to figure out how to plug my new processes into my CRM as much as possible," Tim says.

"Yes!" Barry says, lifting his glass to toast Tim. "We can go over those next week. So that's the CRM component. Our other big topic under processes is implementing processes and improving them over time. This part won't be actionable for you for a while, but you still need to be aware of it."

Tim looks at Wendy. "Wendy, can I send you my outlined processes after this meeting? Maybe you can start thinking about how to integrate them with our CRM."

"Of course," she says, standing. "I'll get out of your hair for now. Barry, it was very nice to meet you. Can I get your information from Tim so I can contact you about your CRM expert?"

"Absolutely," Barry says as Tim scribbles on a sticky note for Wendy.

As Wendy shuts the door, Barry sets his glass down firmly off camera. "All right, Tim, so let's talk about implementing processes," he says.

Tim creates a new heading in his notes.

"First, I want you to know it's possible to make these changes at any stage," Barry says. "The earlier, the better, because as your business grows, making changes becomes more painful. But I've worked with companies over a hundred years old that needed to reorganize their processes around a new vision. It's never too late to get things right."

Tim's eyes widen. "A *hundred* years old?"

"Yep," Barry says with a grin. "And here's the thing—getting started on systems and processes requires a mentality shift. Early on, you're just figuring things out. But once you see what works, you need to codify it. Document it. Turn it into a process. It might take two or three times longer to complete the task as you implement the process, but you'll save thousands of hours later as you are able to get others to do the process while you focus on working on your business. That's how you build consistency and scale your business."

Tim hums. "Right. It's about not just doing things—it's about turning those things into repeatable steps."

"Exactly," Barry says. "You want to get the process as exact and prescriptive as possible. Remove wiggle room so the team will do it right the first time, and later you can automate parts of the process so it moves more quickly."

"Quick is good," Tim says.

"Absolutely," Barry says. "And once you've built that process, you need to make sure everyone follows it. No one is too good for the process. That's where Wendy comes in."

"Right," Tim agrees, brushing crumbs off his shirt. "Even I am not exempt."

"I always personally check our system before answering a question or solving a problem," Barry says. "If something's missing, I direct people back to the process. It's how you ensure scalability. And, of course, you also have to know how the process works. To shift gears a little, how do you know if a process is working?" Barry says.

"Uh," Tim says, "if it works?"

Barry laughs. "I should say, if it's working *well*. The first thing I always ask is, to what percentage would you say your process is well defined and well executed? Is it 70 percent? 100 percent? It's important to define what success looks like."

Tim nods. "Yeah, okay. How do you measure that? What are the metrics?"

"How much of your process has clear, prescriptive directions that are easily understood and accessible by the team?" Barry asks. "How well trained are they to follow those steps? How well designed are those steps so that, if they're followed, the process will be successful?"

Barry pauses, glancing thoughtfully away. "A lot of business owners hesitate to define their processes because they feel like they don't have all the details figured out yet. But here's the thing—you don't need perfection. Don't let the perfect be the enemy of the good. Get started, define the process, and test it. If it works, great. If it doesn't, you can always tweak it along the way."

Tim nods, draining his cup as Barry continues.

"If you get a process that works 80 percent of the time, that's good enough to move on. You'll curate and improve it as you go. The key is consistency—every time your team works with the process, they get better at it. That's how you continuously improve."

Tim types this into his notes. "You have to get started somewhere and be willing to refine things as you go."

Barry nods, grabbing some more of his snack. Tim sees now that he's eating pretzel sticks. "Exactly. The consistency compounds over time. If you get 1 percent better every day, those improvements add up fast. You'll compound to a 3,700 percent improvement in one year. And it's not just about you—it's about partnering with your team. Let them provide feedback, like 'Hey, step three isn't working as well as it should' or 'Sometimes, step four causes a bottleneck.' Involve them in refining the process."

"So, the process needs to involve feedback, just like everything else in the company," Tim says, writing this down.

"Absolutely," Barry says. "It's critical that your team has a major role in defining the process. If you work *with* your team, not only does the process improve, but it also becomes something they take ownership of. I know that's an idea I've reiterated again and again, but it's a very important one. Ownership sets a baseline that guarantees results. And once you have that foundational layer, you can move on to other aspects of the business, like automation, which we'll talk about next week.

"You also have to regularly step back and ask yourself, *Is this still working?*" Barry says as Tim continues typing. "*Does it align with our vision? How do we scale it?* You have to take the time to work *on* the business, not just in it. That's how you avoid getting trapped in the daily grind."

Tim grimaces as he finishes typing a sentence. "That's easier said than done, though."

"True, but it's the only way to build a business that works for you, not the other way around," Barry says. "Like we talked about last week, if you don't put systems in place, you end up trapped—working eighty or ninety hours a week, missing out on family time, and never enjoying the journey."

Tim sighs, looking out the window at the drizzle for a moment before turning back to Barry and his sun-drenched world. "Yeah, I know that all too well. I can see how important all of this is."

Barry grins. "Great. I'd better run here—my wife and I have a wine tasting scheduled for two thirty."

"Rough life," Tim says. "Have a great time. Drink some pinot noir for me."

"Will do," Barry says with a laugh. "Let's review your CRM implementation next week. Then we can dive into automation."

Chapter 10 Summary

Scalable Business Framework: Processes and CRMs

Time Management Matrix

	Urgent	**Not Urgent**
Important	Urgent and important (crisis)	Not urgent but important (focus here)
Not Important	Urgent but not important (time waster)	Not urgent and not important (no value)

Sales Process and CRM Implementation
- Address inconsistent data gathering and lack of sales pipeline visibility.
- Identify and eliminate "pipeline ignorance" and "lagging pipeline" issues.
- Standardize processes to improve client documentation and follow-up.

CRM Technology and Process Integration
- Balance CRM technology with well-defined sales processes.
- Customize CRM to align with business needs and operational workflows.
- Use CRM validation rules to enforce data consistency and track sales progress.

Strategic Business Improvements
- Address latent pain points and focus on long-term benefits beyond immediate ROI.
- Codify and refine successful strategies for consistency and repeatability.
- Involve the team in process refinement to ensure adoption and effectiveness.

Learn more about processes and CRMs at ScalableBusinessFramework.com.

Chapter 11

Automation

Tim spots Barry walking into the coffee shop, his laid-back stride just a bit faster than usual. Tim has managed to arrive first and get them both coffees. Today, La Chance is bedecked in green shamrocks and garlands, and Tim has a bag of Robin's muffins waiting on the table.

As Barry nears, Tim realizes he's holding an oblong gift bag along with his gym duffel. Sliding into the seat across from Tim, Barry grins and places the gift bag on the table.

"I couldn't come back from Napa empty-handed," he says. "Thought you and your wife might enjoy this."

Tim slides the bottle out of the bag. "Pinot noir! Hey, thanks, Barry. This is Robin's favorite." He scans the wine label, already imagining a relaxed evening with her. They've been making a point to get a sitter and have a date night at least once a month.

"Robin actually sent something for you, too," Tim says, taking the muffins out of the bag. Barry's face lights up.

"Excellent," he says. "And what's in this mug? Not Hot for Cupid, I hope?"

"No," Tim says, making a face. "Never again. Although there was an interesting Saint Paddy's drink up there with boiled cabbage . . ."

"I'm good! This looks great, thank you very much," Barry says, seizing his mug with gusto. "Shall we get to the topic at hand?"

Tim, laughing, starts opening his laptop.

"Actually," Barry says, "before we talk about automation, I want to take a step back. A few weeks ago, you talked about getting your team's input on implementing new processes. I'm assuming you've had some time to do that now. How did it go?"

Tim sighs and rubs the back of his neck. "It was eye-opening. I thought the new sales process was clear, but once I brought it to the team, it became obvious there were gaps I hadn't noticed."

Barry nods, a slight smile on his face. "Clarity on paper doesn't always mean clarity in practice. What gaps came up?"

Tim shifts forward, resting his elbows on the table. "Well, one part of the process was handling client follow-ups. I assumed everyone agreed that we should send detailed follow-ups within forty-eight hours, but Jake—our operations guy—pushed back. He said our system makes that timeframe unrealistic unless we cut back on how much detail we ask for. He even suggested dropping the forty-eight-hour rule altogether. It led to a bit of a debate."

Barry raises an eyebrow as he peels the wrapper off his muffin. "Sounds like a healthy disagreement. How did the team handle it?"

Tim exhales sharply. "At first, it got tense. Some people felt Jake was nitpicking, but he made valid points. Others wanted to stick to the original plan because it seemed 'good enough.' I realized we weren't really aligned as a team."

Barry leans forward, his tone thoughtful. "That's a common challenge. When a process is designed top-down, you get exactly that—disagreement and misalignment. But that's why you're doing the work of including the team now."

Tim taps his pen on the table, thinking. "Right, and that's already made for a much more cooperative culture. I took a step back and asked everyone to walk through the process step by step. We mapped out where things broke down and brainstormed a solution. Jake's feedback actually made the process stronger. We adjusted the follow-up time frame to seventy-two hours for now and built in a checklist of what to prioritize. It seemed to get buy-in from the whole team in the end."

Barry smiles, leaning back again. "That's a great approach. By listening to the team, you got to the root of the issue and improved the process. What else did you learn from that experience?"

Tim pauses, then nods. "That even the best ideas need refining. And I saw firsthand how much better things work when the team has ownership. They helped build the process instead of just following orders, and that makes them feel more invested."

Barry smiles. "That horizontal input is what creates accuracy and ownership. Involving your team guarantees their investment. Processes can't survive without that."

Tim sits back and crosses his arms. "Yeah, I get it now. A top-down approach might seem faster, but it doesn't hold up."

Barry tilts his head, his tone more serious now. "It's a lesson every leader learns eventually. So, what's your next step?"

Tim straightens up, also reaching over to grab a muffin. "We'll test this new process for a month, gather data, and refine it," he says. "I also want to hold regular check-ins to make sure everyone's still aligned."

Barry nods approvingly. "Smart move. Processes are never one-and-done—they're living things. Keep the lines of communication open, and you'll see the results. Now, let's move on to the topic of the day. Have you made any progress building this into your CRM?"

Tim leans forward. "Yes. Wendy and I spent a full day mapping out every key stage of our sales process and pinpointing where we need those data checkpoints to ensure accuracy." He opens his laptop. "Here, let me share this spreadsheet with you. It's a good spreadsheet, I promise."

"I'm sure it is," Barry says, pulling out a tablet. He clicks on the email as it arrives and starts scrolling.

"I set up validation rules at each critical stage," Tim explains. "For example, when a prospect goes from discovery to proposal, the system now checks whether the team has filled in the client's goals, timeline, and budget. If any of those are missing, they can't proceed to the next step. That way, no one's moving forward with half-baked info."

"Good idea," Barry says.

"For on-site visits, Wendy and I implemented a clear recordkeeping method to capture all details accurately, including automated follow-ups in our CRM to ensure consistency and efficiency."

"Wow!" Barry says. "You've been busy."

"Got to get those systems and processes in place," Tim says, taking a bite of a muffin.

"Did you have a chance to run this past your team, or has it just been you and Wendy so far?"

Tim nods. "Yes. Wendy tested the CRM updates with a few team members, and it's been seamless. Once we've finalized everything, we'll have a meeting with everyone involved to explain the changes and get feedback."

"A test phase sounds like a good idea," Barry says.

"We just wanted to make sure the rollout was as easy as possible for everyone," Tim says. "I also took your advice and modeled our quote tracking after The Spice Mart's process. Each on-site visit now logs a quote under the main opportunity to track our estimates so we have full visibility and can capture more data. It's a relief to know nothing is falling through the cracks."

Barry scrolls through the spreadsheet, then looks up at Tim. "That's fantastic," he says. "You're addressing the big pain points right out of the gate. One small suggestion: What do you think about setting up a weekly review session with Wendy to go over data quality and process adherence? Over time, team members sometimes start taking shortcuts, or you might need to adjust the CRM requirements. A check-in will help catch any inconsistencies early."

Tim quickly types this into his notes. "Good point. A weekly review will help keep things sharp. I'll make sure it's on the calendar."

Barry adds, "Another thought—set up a feedback loop in the CRM. Let your team easily log any issues or suggestions so they're empowered to flag things in real time. It'll help keep them engaged and give you a heads-up about any friction points."

Tim nods. "I like that. I'll add a simple feedback form directly in the CRM for them."

Barry smiles. "So, tell me. Have you made any discoveries so far with your test group?"

Tim leans back, chuckling. "Yeah, honestly, it's revealing some interesting trends already. For example, we've noticed that deals with delayed proposals often lack detailed goal and budget information. That alone has been eye-opening, and it's shown us where we need to ask more targeted questions up front."

Barry grins. "That's great. That's the beauty of integrating these checkpoints. Every data point tells a story, and over time, you'll spot patterns you never saw before. This kind of visibility allows you to be proactive instead of reactive."

Tim nods. "Wendy is loving it. With the CRM capturing all this information, she's able to give the team more targeted support, knowing exactly where they're stuck. I'm loving it because I know the results are going to be consistently high quality. It's a big relief to see the system taking shape like this."

Barry nods as the espresso machine whirs in the background. "I'm thrilled to hear it's already making a difference. The CRM customizations will be a big asset as you scale. Just remember—these processes are living structures. Make it a habit to step back every so often and ask if they're still serving your needs. The stronger your foundation, the easier it'll be to adjust as you grow."

Tim types the advice into his notes, nodding. "That's exactly what we'll do. I want this to be a tool that grows with us."

"Fabulous," Barry says. "Now that we've laid a solid foundation with processes and some CRM customizations, let's dive into the second core principle of the framework: automation. I've been thinking a lot about your body analogy; that was really a stroke of genius, Tim. It works on so many levels."

"I'm just that good," Tim says with a lopsided grin.

"Naturally," Barry says, smiling too. "Now, if the systems and processes are the musculoskeletal system, do you remember what system automation is?"

Tim ponders this, tapping a finger on his arm. "I remember you saying it's like all the automatic processes that happen in the body," he says. "Like your heartbeat and stuff."

"Right," Barry confirms. "Think of automation like the autonomic nervous system in your body. It controls things like your respiratory rate, heart rate, breathing, and digestion—all those critical passive functions that keep you alive."

Tim chuckles. "Right. I'm glad I don't have to focus on digesting every time I eat."

"Me too," Barry says, laughing. "It would be impossible to get anything done, right? Speaking of which, let's talk about the advantages of having automatic functions in your business as well as your body. The way I see it, there are two big advantages, and the first one is efficiency."

As Barry talks, one foot propped up on his knee, Tim starts a list.

"A lot of businesses have critical tasks that aren't automated," Barry explains. Behind him, a cluster of parents with kids makes a beeline for the bathroom. "They have to consciously think through those things every single day. This is not efficient for a few reasons. It's like trying to have a conversation while manually controlling your breathing. Do you think you could do a better job digesting or pumping blood than your body does automatically?"

"Oh, definitely not," Tim says.

"Right," Barry says. "Automation is about efficiency—getting things done faster and better. Let's say your team has to spend time building quote documents, writing the same types of emails, or trying to remember what tasks are next in a sales cycle. At this point, we have technology that handles those tasks better than any person can. It's more efficient to put the process in place and automate what can be automated. Automation ensures that the right things get done at the right time without anyone having to worry about it."

"Yeah, that sounds great," Tim says.

"What about it sounds great?" Barry asks.

Tim looks up in surprise. "Well, it makes work more efficient, like you said. That's for sure. But also, it frees up time for tasks that can't be automated."

"Exactly!" says Barry exuberantly, doing a little fist bump in the air. "If you automate what you can, you remove distractions that don't need to occupy your time or your team's time. Instead, everyone can focus on more overarching tasks—things that actually drive the business forward. In other words, automation makes your team more *effective*. Effectiveness is the second big advantage of automation.

"By taking low-value tasks off their plates and your own plate, you free everyone up to focus on activities that truly move the needle," Barry says as Tim types. "No one can function at a higher level if you're bogged down by those repetitive but essential tasks, like digesting food or tracking client follow-up dates or what have you."

Tim nods. "Yeah, I think it was a big part of my own work-life integration woes."

"It is for so many of my clients," Barry says. "Automation is a huge time-saver—it helps with efficiency. But it also helps with effectiveness in several ways. It reduces demand for your time and your mental load. It takes care of those basic functions so you can focus on bigger things."

"I'll sign up for anything that makes my job easier," Tim says. "I hate thinking about the minutiae anyway."

"Many business owners do," Barry says. "A lot of people don't realize how transformative automation can be for their business. They think of it as just a bonus feature, but it's not. It truly changes everything. It doesn't just save a few minutes here and there. Automation lets you elevate your business and focus on more big-picture tasks—the stuff only you can contribute."

"The time and attention savings extends to your team as well," Barry explains as Tim sits back, listening. "You identify key milestones and tasks for your team, then automate those lower-level tasks, freeing your people up to focus on higher-value work. When your team isn't bogged down with mundane, repetitive tasks—like writing emails, generating quotes, or remembering task reminders—they can focus on adding real value."

Barry starts breaking his muffin into pieces as he talks. "Some business owners balk at automating because they're worried about losing the human connection," he says, "but it doesn't mean removing the human element. It's about spending less time on the tasks that don't add value so your team has more time to focus on the personal interactions that do. You can strike the right balance."

Tim taps a note into his laptop. "Great. And that incorporates really well with systems and processes."

"Absolutely," Barry says, taking a moment to down a piece of muffin. "These get better every time. Please thank Robin for me."

"Careful, or she'll start sending them every week," Tim says with a laugh.

"Well, since we only have one week left to cover the SBF, that wouldn't be so bad, would it?" Barry asks. "Although, truth be told, I could easily eat these every week."

Tim feels a lead weight settle in his stomach. "One more week?" he says.

Barry gives Tim a searching look. "Don't look so shocked, Tim," he says. "Think of how much things have changed already. Think of how much you're learning now. It will only take me one more session to finish teaching you about the Scalable Business Framework, sure, but that doesn't mean we'll never see each other again."

"Okay," Tim says, somewhat mollified.

"Now, there's one more angle to effectiveness here," Barry says, scooting forward to allow the parents and children to file past and crowd around a table near the front of the store. "That's guaranteed outcomes. When you have solid processes and you layer automation on top of them, you start to have more consistent outcomes. That's what makes the whole business operation more reliable."

Tim types a few more notes. "Just like how systems and processes provide more consistent outcomes?" he asks.

"That's right," Barry says. "If your process has an 80 percent success rate, automation can bump that up to 90 or even 95 percent. It removes human error from those routine tasks, making everything run more smoothly. It improves quality by ensuring the basic tasks are done consistently."

"Okay," Tim says. "That makes sense."

"One more advantage to discuss," Barry says. "Growth. When you create space for everyone to think about what really matters, you're also creating space for everyone to focus on growing and scaling the company. The whole team can now focus on what's important and not just what's urgent. With processes automated and efficient and everyone working effectively, scalability improves a lot. You're no longer bogged down by repetitive tasks—you're freed up to focus on growth."

Tim writes this down, then takes a look at his notes.

Automation Advantages
1. Efficiency (faster, better)
2. Effectiveness
3. Time and attention savings = more opportunities to add real value for both leader and team
4. Growth

Tim looks back up at Barry and nods.

"Okay, I think I've got it," he says. "This sounds amazing, honestly. I think this is part of the reason I struggled so much with scaling before."

"Very likely so," Barry says. "Now, let's talk prerequisites for a second."

"There are always prerequisites," Tim says, smiling.

"Oh, yes," Barry says sagely. "First, you have to have a good process in place. Automation is only as good as the process it's built on. If you automate a bad process, you just get bad results faster. But if you automate a good process, it creates scalability."

Tim nods. "Well, luckily, I've just spent all this time building good processes."

"Right," Barry says, his eyes sparkling. "So you've fulfilled the prerequisites already. Look at that."

"It's almost like we're going in a specific order for a reason," Tim says with a chuckle. Barry winks and takes the opportunity to down a bite-sized piece of muffin, and Tim glances out the window, where a group of businesspeople are heading somewhere together, long coats flapping in the cool breeze.

"Now that we've laid the groundwork for automation," Barry says after a few seconds, "let's talk about finding parts of processes to automate."

"Yes," Tim says, starting a new heading in his notes.

"When we look at processes, we ask a few key questions. The first is, what can we automate around the constraints?"

"What do you mean by that?" Tim asks.

"Every business will develop constraints and bottlenecks as it grows," Barry explains. "Some of those may be inevitable. One example is an approval process. Typically, it's handled through email, and every item is sent for approval. But as the company grows, this becomes unmanageable."

"Oh," Tim says. "Yeah, that sounds familiar."

"When those difficulties arise, it's important to use automation to streamline and focus the data so you can minimize the impact of that bottleneck," Barry says, pausing to grin at a passing man in a flannel shirt and jeans, who waves as though he knows Barry. Which he probably does.

"If you build automation that automatically identifies certain records above a threshold for approval and submits them to a regional or divisional approver, things move a lot faster," Barry says. "You can then automate the data flow to show approvals in one place instead of being frustrated because they get lost in an inbox."

"Got it," Tim says.

"There are other considerations as well," Barry says. "What's repeatable? What outcome do we want? What data do we need? What communication needs to be automated? And, most importantly, what *behaviors* can we automate?"

Tim's brain buzzes with ideas. "Behaviors . . . just like integrating a helpful reminder into a process."

"Exactly," Barry says. "We dive into the process and identify what's slowing the team down. We ask if there are routine tasks—like emailing, building quotes, or managing projects—that are eating into their time. What can we automate to take it off their plate?"

"What are the first candidates, typically?" Tim asks, eating the last bite of his muffin and wondering just how much he can automate. He'd love to automate it all.

"Oh, boring stuff like building quote documents or writing repetitive emails," Barry says. "Let's take a salesperson following up on a project. Normally, they have to manually track who they need to follow up with and write a new email every time. Instead, using a CRM, we can set up an automated reminder. The salesperson can then log into the system, see the reminder, and access a pre-built email template—90 percent of what they need to say is already there. They can customize it with personal touches, but the heavy lifting is done for them."

Tim types a few notes, his brow furrowing slightly, then looks up at Barry. "Okay," he says.

"You look a little confused," Barry says, eyebrows raised as he helps himself to more of his muffin.

"Well," Tim says, feeling sheepish, "When you talked about automation, I thought of something a lot more sophisticated than a reminder with an email template. My salespeople already use templates, but I can see how they mesh well with the reminders . . ." He scratches his chin. "It just seems kind of . . . anticlimactic?"

Barry chuckles. "You were picturing an army of robots doing your jobs for you, weren't you?"

"Maybe," Tim says with a grin. One of the children at the front table begins to cry, and the child's mother hands her a toy, shushing her.

"That's a common misconception," Barry says, swirling the content of his mug. "When people hear 'automation,' they imagine complex AI, expensive systems integration, or custom code. But that's not always necessary or even smart. We can have a massive impact on a business with simple automation principles using the CRM you're already paying for. Something as straightforward as automating task reminders or using email templates can dramatically improve efficiency. You don't need a high-end system to start automating; it's about *finding the right tasks* to automate. When you automate those routine, repetitive tasks, you create space for your team to do what they do best—add value to the client."

Tim mulls this over. "Okay, okay. Simple and quick is good."

"That's the right idea," Barry says. "And another key here is that it's not about replacing people—it's about *supporting* them. With the automation I just described, your sales team doesn't have to consult some spreadsheet filled with dates for their follow-up schedule, and they don't have to copy and paste templates over and over. Instead they can focus on building relationships and adding value. *That's* where automation really shines."

Tim sits back, nodding. "Yeah," he says. "That makes sense. No robot army for me, I guess."

"Hey, give it another twenty years," Barry says, smiling. "You never know. But for now, these simple automations also ensure consistency. For example, if you build a quote in Excel manually every time, you're leaving room for errors or inconsistencies. But if you automate that process with a standardized template, you ensure that 95 percent of the quote is accurate, and the team only needs to customize the last 5 percent for each client."

Tim nods. "I've definitely spent more time than I should formatting quote documents."

Barry grins. "We've all been there. Now, let's move along to the next phase. Let's say you've identified a part of a task that you can automate. Next, you have to think about the downstream impact and ensure the automation works for everyone downstream of the task."

"Downstream impact?" Tim asks, looking up.

"Yes," Barry says. "For example, when you pass a job to the service team, how can we ensure they have all the information they need to be successful? The more data we can automate and pass along, the smoother everything runs. It's about making life easier for everyone involved."

"Oookay," Tim says. "So even if the automation is in the sales process, it isn't just for the sales team. It impacts everything that comes after sales."

"Right," Barry says. "You're not just automating one task. You're automating the flow of information through the entire business."

"Automating the flow of information," Tim says, writing this down. "I like that."

"Me too, Tim," Barry says, smiling. "For example, when we pass a job over to the service team, how can we ensure they don't have to manually input that data again? What can we automate to make sure everything flows seamlessly?"

"That," Tim says, sitting back in his chair, "is huge." He can now see how big an impact automation could have on FastTrack.

Barry's smile widens. "Sure is. Let me give you a practical example from Charis Strategies. At one point, we realized that following up on a project two or three weeks after it was sold drastically reduces the chance of an expectation gap at the end of the project."

Tim cocks his head. "Expectation gap?"

Barry nods. "Yeah. Imagine you kick off a project, and eight or nine weeks go by. Then, when you're wrapping up, the client says, 'I didn't get this thing I wanted.' That creates a gap between what the client expected and what was delivered."

"Ah, got it," Tim says, sipping his drink. "I suppose my business is susceptible to those too."

"Many are," Barry says. "In service businesses especially, managing expectations is everything. But if you follow up a few weeks in and ask how things are going, you can catch those issues early. We found that by automating a simple follow-up reminder, we could close that gap."

Tim's eyes light up. "That's genius. So, how did you do it?"

"We built a simple automation," Barry says. "Three weeks after a project is sold, the salesperson gets a pop-up reminder to follow up with the client. There's an email template ready to go. The salesperson can customize it with personal touches, but 90 percent of the work is already done. No sticky notes, no relying on memory. The system runs that critical part of the process."

Tim smiles. "Email templates again, huh?"

Barry shrugs, palms facing up. "Again, automation doesn't have to be complicated. It's about identifying critical behaviors and building simple systems to support them. In this case, a simple, fast automated task drastically improved our team's success by ensuring follow-ups happened at the right time."

Tim taps a few more notes into his laptop. "I can see how that would be a huge help. I guess I need a few automatic email templates myself."

Barry looks at Tim. "I've thought of an example that doesn't involve email templates." He says, his eyes sparkling.

"Now you're talking," Tim says. "Let's hear it." Behind Barry, the door opens to admit a group of college students.

"This is from a client we worked with called INB," Barry says. "Similar to FastTrack, INB ran a business with a large number of technicians performing on-site services. INB managed all of their processes in spreadsheets including job assignments and routing."

"The dreaded spreadsheet method," Tim says, nodding seriously. "Rookie mistake."

Barry laughs. "You hit the nail on the head. INB's business exploded, and they weren't organized enough to handle it. They were drowning. We jumped in and helped them implement field service automation, optimizing their operations, and a big part of that was automating task assignments. Their techs were passing each other on the road to different jobs, wasting time. So, when we automated the job assignment process, we made sure the closest qualified technician to the job got assigned. It saved them an incredible amount of time."

Tim whistles softly. "That's a big win," he says, drawing his sweater closer momentarily as a couple opens the door to La Chance wide, letting in a big gust of cool air. "How does that work, exactly?"

"The jobs are scheduled ahead of time," Barry explains. "The automated system finds the right tech whose previous job is closest to the newly scheduled job. It only schedules techs whose skills qualify for that type of job, so the result is minimized travel time and cost as well as the right tech at the right job."

"Sounds like a perfect solution," says Tim.

"It was," Barry says. "And then they got lucky. One of INB's largest vendors, Horizon, offered them the chance to integrate directly with their system. Horizon wanted to assign them jobs automatically, and because we'd already built a robust process and automation system, all we had to do was build the integration. Now the Horizon system assigns jobs directly to INB's team with no human involvement necessary. That's a windfall INB wouldn't have been able to handle if they hadn't automated their processes. That's return on luck."

Tim leans back in his chair, macchiato in hand. "Talk about scalability."

"Exactly," Barry says brightly. "It was a huge win for them. That's the power of automation. You're making things easier today, but you're also preparing for future growth. Automation ensures you can handle the opportunities that come your way without drowning in the process."

Barry glances at his watch, pauses to down the rest of his coffee, then looks at Tim. "Now, Tim, I have to run—I've got an appointment. But I'm sure you can guess what your homework is."

"Automate identified processes," Tim says quickly, saving his notes. "I've already drafted an email to Wendy with my notes from this meeting linked. What's the best way to get started?"

"You're already on the right track," Barry says. "Working with your team to identify low-value, manual tasks is the best place to start; they can tell you what tasks prevent them from focusing on adding the most value." His eyes brighten, and he looks at Tim. "One area that could really use this is your new goal of cutting down follow-up time from seventy-two hours to forty-eight hours. You could try asking the employee who had the feedback about the follow-up timeframe to pitch in on which tasks could be automated."

"Great idea," Tim says. "I'll run that by Jake."

"Remember to start with simple items and pick just a few," Barry says. "You don't want to try to boil the ocean—start with a small pot."

Tim nods, typing more notes as Barry continues.

"If you have multiple tools, see what options you have to use automation to bring the datasets together," Barry says, ticking items off on his fingers. "That saves time and effort."

"Wait," Tim says, looking up. "What do you mean by that?"

"As companies grow, they tend to onboard new tool after new tool," Barry explains. "Marketing automation tools, job tracking tools, job assignment tools...after a while, they suddenly have a dozen tools and can't track the business across all of them. It's best practice to combine as many tools as possible and use automation to integrate and sync the data to a single source of truth for visibility and decision-making. Otherwise, you'll be limited in the types of decisions you can make."

"Oh," Tim says. "Got it. Yeah, I'll watch out for that."

"Finally, if you don't know what to automate first, use reporting to decide," Barry says, "Where is your team the slowest? Where are they bogged down? Look there for potential automation solutions. Your team will thank you." He quickly eats the last piece of his muffin.

"Got it," Tim says, reviewing what he's just written.

How to Start Automating
1. Identify a few simple, manual tasks that are bottlenecking the team.
2. Examine options to bring data together.
3. Use reporting to identify processes to automate.

"Excellent," Barry says, standing up. "I'm looking forward to hearing all about your progress with automation next week. And once you've got the automation in place, the next step is visibility. That means tracking the impact of everything you've automated."

"Great," Tim says, stuffing his laptop back into his bag. "I do see a lot of stuff about data here . . . I'm guessing we'll talk about that next week."

"You bet," Barry says.

"And thanks again for the wine," Tim says. "I can't wait to share it with Robin. Please take the rest of the muffins home with you."

"Oh, thanks a lot!" Barry says. "These make a great post-workout snack. I'll see you next week, Tim. Can't wait to talk about visibility."

Chapter 11 Summary

Scalable Business Framework—Automation

Automation Advantages
- Efficiency—faster, better
- Effectiveness
- Time and attention savings = more opportunities to add real value for both leader and team
- Easier growth

How to Start Automating
- Identify a few simple, manual tasks that are bottlenecking the team.
- Examine options to bring data together.
- Use reporting to identify processes to automate.

Strategic Implementation
- Assess downstream impacts before implementing automation.
- Evaluate data integration options for seamless workflow improvements.
- Prioritize automation efforts based on measurable inefficiencies.

Learn more about automation at ScalableBusinessFramework.com.

Chapter 12

Visibility

Tim walks into La Chance, taking off his sunglasses and blinking to adjust after the bright sunlight. The coffee shop is an explosion of green today, complete with an Irish tune playing over the speaker system. The management seems to have put up even more decorations over the past week.

Tim sees Barry sitting in his usual spot, saying goodbye to a woman in a tan trench coat. Barry sits back in his chair and waves as Tim sets his bag down.

"Harper's got your order at the counter," Barry says by way of greeting.

"Oh, thank you," Tim says. "Do you need anything else? Looks like you've been here for a minute."

"I might run to the restroom while you set up," Barry stands. He's wearing a green workout shirt.

Tim grabs his coffee, orders two Irish soda breads in lieu of the giant frosted shamrock cookies, and hauls out his laptop. He opens up his notes and scrolls down, looking at everything he has learned. A smile creeps across his face as he thinks about how much has changed already.

"What are you reading?"

Tim lets out an involuntary yelp and looks up. Barry has snuck up behind him and is now laughing.

"Sorry, sorry." Barry waves his hands as he sits down, nudging his gym duffel to the side with one foot. "So, tell me about automation, my friend. What did you and Wendy decide on?"

Tim shakes his head. "You just took years off my life."

"I doubt that," Barry says, still laughing.

"Okay, well, if you promise never to do that again, I'll share this spreadsheet with you." Tim gestures to his laptop.

"I promise," Barry says solemnly, sliding his tablet out of his bag. "And, hey, thanks for grabbing those." He gestures to the soda bread. "Looks delicious. By the way, how was that first baseball game?"

"The kids killed it!" Tim says. "I think I embarrassed them by cheering too much. I might have gone a little hoarse." He laughs. "I was just excited to be there, you know?"

"I completely understand," Barry says, smiling as Tim sends him the spreadsheet link.

"Diving into last week's homework really shifted my perspective," Tim says. "Wendy and I didn't just identify tasks to automate—we also saw how automation could tie different parts of the business together in ways I hadn't considered. Oh, but before we talk about that, I want to loop back to CRM customization for a second."

"Sure," Barry says. "Last week, you were still testing. Have you deployed the changes?"

"Yes!" Tim says excitedly. "And it's already paying off. It's making the changes we already implemented work much more seamlessly. I can see how it will stop things from falling through the cracks."

"Fantastic, Tim," Barry says, turning to the new spreadsheet. "So glad to hear that. Now, tell me about this."

"Right—automation," Tim says. "We pinpointed tasks that were repetitive and time-consuming. Take follow-ups, for example, since we were already trying to shorten that window from seventy-two to forty-eight hours."

"Yes, I remember," Barry says. "How did that go?"

"Surprisingly well," Tim says. "We've actually already implemented automated reminders for follow-ups. Before, it was a manual task—sales reps had to rely on sticky notes or memory to track follow-ups. Now our CRM generates automatic reminders twenty-four hours after an initial client contact."

"That's a great approach," Barry says, nodding. "And how's that working out so far?"

Tim grins. "Well, we've only been using it for a few days, but it's made a huge difference. The reps have already noticed how much easier it is to stay on top of their pipelines, and we've shortened the follow-up period to more like thirty-six hours. Jake is thrilled!"

"So you beat your goal. That's wonderful," Barry says, using his tablet to scroll through the spreadsheet Tim shared. "I see here that you did a follow-up email template as well."

"Those have also already been a huge time-saver," Tim says. "They still allow for customization, like you suggested, but the team really likes that the heavy lifting is done ahead of time."

Barry nods in approval. "Sounds like you've nailed the basics. Any other areas you tackled?"

"We also looked at how we hand off information from sales to our service team," Tim says. "That's where we've historically had some bottlenecks. Wendy created a system where key job data—like scope, deadlines, and client expectations—gets automatically transferred into the project management system as soon as a deal closes. No more manual data entry!"

Barry's face lights up. "That's huge, Tim. You've eliminated a major point of friction."

Tim sighs happily. "It's early, but I can already see how much smoother the process is going to be," he says. "The service team's feedback has been positive so far."

"Excellent," Barry says, propping his tablet up on its stand. "Automation isn't just about efficiency; it's about making the entire business flow better. It sounds like you really absorbed that."

Tim leans forward. "Speaking of flow, one thing I realized during this process is how much automation can impact team morale," he says. "I wasn't expecting that exactly, but it's a huge bonus. Taking repetitive tasks off their plates really changed the mood. The team feels more energized to focus on client relationships and creative problem-solving. It's like giving them permission to work on what they actually care about."

Barry gives Tim a little toast with his coffee mug. "That's one of the hidden benefits of automation," he says. "When you free people from mundane tasks, you give them the bandwidth to bring more value to the table. And that value flows directly back to the business."

"Right," Tim says, nodding. "I also went ahead and scheduled those weekly review sessions with Wendy to assess data quality and process adherence, like we discussed. And it was a good thing we did, too. We had our first one already, and we caught a recurring issue where client contact info wasn't being updated."

"Uh-oh," Barry says.

"Yeah," Tim agrees. "One of the entries we flagged was for an older client, Mr. Jenkins. Turns out he moved into a new home six months ago, and we didn't have his new address. That could have been a disaster if we'd sent equipment to his old place. Catching it in time saved us a headache and showed Mr. Jenkins's family we were on top of things."

"That's a relief," Barry says. "Must have felt great."

"It did," Tim says. "The family was grateful, and it gave me a lot of confidence in how useful these reviews will be. I also added a feedback loop in the CRM with a simple form for team members to log issues and suggestions. We've actually already had a few great ideas come through that way."

"Oh, yeah?" Barry says. "Like what?"

"Well, one of the techs suggested adding a drop-down menu for common service notes," Tim says. "But my favorite so far was from one of our salespeople—she developed a way to streamline scheduling by integrating it with our inventory system. We've already implemented it, and it's saving us a ton of back-and-forth with the warehouse."

"It's amazing what happens when people feel empowered to share their ideas," Barry says.

Tim's smile widens. "Couldn't agree more. So, what's next?"

"We've talked about processes and automation, but now we come to the third critical component of the Scalable Business Framework: visibility," Barry says. "Within the framework, visibility ties everything together. Once you've got the right processes and automation in place, it allows you to track how those systems are performing."

"Sounds good," Tim says. He takes an experimental sip of his macchiato and burns his tongue. Smacking his lips, he puts the mug back down.

"Now, like the other components of the SBF, visibility has several specific benefits," Barry says. "First, visibility empowers us to adjust. Think of it as the sensory system of your business."

"Man, you've really run with my analogy," Tim says, shaking his head.

"Hey, it was a great idea," Barry says, beaming. "As far as visibility is concerned, just like your body relies on sight, touch, and hearing to navigate the world, your business needs visibility into its operations to make adjustments. It gives you the information you need to adapt as you go. That's the first benefit. As I mentioned before, it's like pulling your hand away from a hot stove—you need to be able to sense what's going on so you can react appropriately."

Tim starts a list in his notes as Barry continues to explain.

"You need the data and insights to understand both your internal processes and external factors," Barry says. "I've worked with businesses that don't have this level of visibility, and they struggle to make the right adjustments. Think about it—how limiting is it to rely on something like a deal spreadsheet to track your sales pipeline? It's static and lacks real-time insights."

"Here we go with the spreadsheets again," Tim says jokingly.

"Hey, you're phasing out the spreadsheets," Barry says with a chuckle. "Anyway, that's where visibility becomes crucial. With the right systems in place, you can see exactly where things are going right—or wrong—and make real-time adjustments. I think the best story for this is the *Titanic*."

"The *Titanic*?" Tim says, surprised.

"It may be over a hundred years old, but it perfectly illustrates the importance of visibility," Barry says, sitting back in his chair, looking relaxed. "The *Titanic* was the best-engineered ship of its time—infamously considered unsinkable. It had all the amenities and all the design innovations. Two days into its voyage, the crew received a warning about icebergs ahead, but that data didn't make it to the bridge in time. When they finally saw the iceberg, they had thirty-seven seconds to react.[37] And we all know what happened."

"Huh," Tim says.

"The main problem wasn't the ship's design or advanced engineering—it was a *data* issue," Barry says, leaning forward. "The *Titanic* didn't fail because it wasn't well engineered; it failed because the captain and his crew didn't have the data they needed when they needed it. If they'd had the right visibility into the situation, they could've made an adjustment long before it was too late."

Tim nods. "I suppose that's right."

"And that's exactly what happens in businesses," Barry says, spreading his hands. "You might have great processes and automation in place, but if you don't have visibility into what's actually happening, you're flying blind. You can't

---

[37] History.com Editors, "Could the Titanic Disaster Have Been Avoided?," History.com video, A&E Television Networks, May 30, 2012, last updated June 19, 2019, 3 min., 39 sec., https://www.history.com/topics/early-20th-century-us/titanics-achilles-heel-attempt-to-avoid-disaster-video.

make adjustments if you don't know where things are going off track. Once you identify the visibility issues, you can improve your processes and automations and continue to iterate through the Scalable Business Framework."

"Okay, got it," Tim says, writing a few more notes down.

"The second benefit of visibility," Barry says, "is that it creates a single source of truth."

"Sounds like some kind of cult," Tim says skeptically, and Barry laughs.

"Well, okay, it won't give you the secrets of the universe," Barry admits. "But it does act something like an oracle for your business. I actually think this is best described using one problem visibility solves, which is the inability to see data across business functions."

"Like, the inability to see the big picture?" Tim asks, picking up the soda bread and tearing off a piece.

"Basically, yes," Barry says. "As businesses grow, they add new systems or tools to manage different areas. Suddenly, they've got ten different systems running the business. It's impossible to get a clear picture of what's going on because the data is so disconnected. That's why consolidating everything into a single CRM is so important. It brings everything together in one place, giving you real visibility into your entire business."

Barry leans his elbows on the table and looks to the side as he thinks. "Imagine this scenario," he says. "You ask the sales team how much was sold last quarter, and they give you a number. Then you ask the technicians, and they give you a completely different number. Why? Because they're using two different systems, each with its own definitions. That's what I mean by lacking a single source of truth—no one's working off the same data."

"Ohhh," Tim says slowly, chewing the soda bread. It has a pleasant, slightly tangy flavor. "Okay, that I can get behind."

"Good," Barry says. "When Charis Strategies works with clients, we put all data in one system. That way, when management asks how much they sold, they have one number—one source of truth. Everyone in the organization is working from the same set of numbers. That's what visibility does. It gives you a clear picture of the business."

Tim nods, glancing over his notes.

Advantages of Visibility

1. Adaptability
2. Unified information (single source of truth)

"Okay, this makes sense," Tim says, pulling another piece off the soda bread.

"Great," Barry says. "Now, let's talk about the data itself. There are a few types of data we look at in the framework, including lagging and leading indicators. These are two concepts common in economics and data analysis.

"First, we have lagging indicators," he continues. "These are your traditional metrics—what you sold last month, your close rate, your year-over-year comparisons. They reflect past performance. Most people use these metrics to manage the business, but that's like driving by looking at the rearview mirror."

Tim nods. This sounds familiar to him.

"We also have leading indicators. These are the inputs into the process," Barry explains as Tim types. "Leading indicators—like the number of leads and deal close rates—are essential for understanding how your business will perform in the future. For example, how many leads did you get this month? If you know your close rate and how long your sales cycle is, you can predict how many deals you'll close three months from now. Leading indicators help you forecast and adjust before it's too late. When you know what inputs (leading indicators) drive the right outcomes (lagging indicators), you get the privilege of driving your business by looking through the windshield instead of in the rearview mirror."

"Okay," Tim says, picking up his coffee and carefully taking a tiny sip. It seems a little cooler now. "So, we've got data that tells us what happened and data that tells us what will happen."

"Exactly," Barry says with a grin. "You're not waiting until the end of the month to see how you did. You're looking at the inputs right now so you can adjust before it's too late."

"Yes, that's a good idea," Tim says.

Barry nods, picking up his soda bread. "Exception management is the third part," he says, tearing off a piece. "It's another common analysis concept. Most processes produce the right outcomes 85 to 95 percent of the time. But there's always that little percentage that falls outside the norm. Those are exceptions. With visibility, we can flag those outliers and expose them to the team for examination."

Tim types another note. "I can see how that would help you find a little issue before it becomes a bigger problem."

"Right," Barry says. "Exception management is powerful because it allows managers to collaborate with their teams and address issues early. When the team knows something is outside the norm, they can act on it, which leads to better results overall."

Tim finishes typing and looks over his new list as Barry chews another bite of soda bread.

Types of Data
1. Lagging indicators
2. Leading indicators
3. Exceptions

The coffee shop is now nearly full, and the whir of the espresso machine and chatter of voices surround the two men. The patrons are wearing a disproportionate amount of green today, and Tim is glad he wore his green dress shirt under his blazer. He has no desire to get pinched.

"Now, whenever you're gathering this data, there are a few practical considerations," Barry says. "First, you have to ask yourself if you're capturing enough detail to make informed decisions. If you don't know why you're winning or losing deals, you can't repeat the wins or avoid the losses. Real visibility is not just about having data—it's about having the *right* data."

Tim types as Barry continues to explain. "This is why a CRM is so valuable. These systems relate the data for you. Without solid architecture, you can capture all the data you want, but it won't have a story to tell you."

"You need a system to structure and contextualize the data so you can maximize your insights," Tim adds.

"You've hit the nail on the head," Barry says, motioning with his hand while holding the soda bread. "Equally, it's about data access. Can you get that data anytime you want, or are you waiting for a report at the end of the month? If your data is spread across nine different systems, how easily can you get the full picture? Can you ensure the right people have access to the data that aligns with their job function?"

Tim pauses, thinking. "That makes sense. You want to have everything available when you need it, not just at limited times."

Barry nods. "That's the power of visibility. And looking at data once a month doesn't give you the whole story. Data velocity matters too. How fast does the data move in your organization? If you're waiting for a report at the end of the month, you're already behind. The more frequently you can access your data, the more responsive you can be in real time. You need to be able to pull up your dashboard and watch what's happening. It's the difference between being proactive and being reactive."

"Hmm," says Tim. "I've never thought about that before."

"That's why we focus on data velocity," Barry says. "We build systems that give managers the ability to check critical metrics in real time so they can make decisions proactively."

Tim nods. "All right, I think I'm getting the full picture now. You need the right data, in the right place, at the right time."

"Exactly," Barry says. "It's all connected. If your data is structured well, if it's available when you need it, and if you're looking at both leading and lagging indicators, you have a full picture of your business. You can make real-time decisions and adjust as needed."

Tim looks at the little list in his notes.

Considerations for Gathering Data
- Data capture
- Data structure
- Data access/availability
- Data velocity

"This is all making a lot of sense," Tim says to Barry. "And it connects well with the CRM automation work from last week. Data will be easier to grab when our processes are streamlined."

"Definitely," Barry says. "You've hit on the core concept of having a good data structure. This is why we use a CRM. That relational model gives us a clear line of sight from top to bottom. It's important to have your data in one place so you can monitor not just what happened in the past but also leading indicators and exceptions in real time."

"Oh, excuse me, Barry," an older man in a suit says as he accidentally bumps Barry's chair. Barry gives him an airy wave with one hand.

"No problem, John," he says. "Still on for lunch next week?"

"Looking forward to it," says the man, tipping his hat to Tim before making his way toward the front of the shop.

"Do you know everyone?" Tim asks in mock exasperation.

"No, but I'm working on it," Barry says jovially. "Now, back to visibility and CRMs. If you're using spreadsheets for reporting, it's a signal that something's missing."

"I get it, I get it," Tim says. "Spreadsheets are the root of all evil."

Barry snorts with laughter. "They can be very useful, but if you're relying on them to run your business, it means your data isn't centralized," he says. "They might indicate that different departments are using different data, and that's a problem. You need a single source of truth."

"Yeah, okay," Tim says. "And that works well with the processes and automation we've already integrated into our CRM."

Barry smiles. "I'd like to tell you about one more key concept of visibility," he says. "I got this idea from Gino Wickman's book *Traction*, where he introduced the Entrepreneurial Operating System (EOS).[38] The idea is that you've got to make sure every team member knows their number. Does every team member know what their success looks like? Do they understand the KPIs that define whether they're successful in their role? And, most importantly, do they have the tools and data at their fingertips to gauge that success?"

Tim's fingers fly as he types. "That makes so much sense," he says. "When each person knows their number, you create accountability."

"Precisely," Barry says. "Everyone has a clear understanding of their role and how it contributes to the success of the business. That's how you build a scalable business—by empowering your team with the right data and visibility."

"Is that my homework, then?" Tim asks.

"Sure is," Barry says. "You'll want to figure out your top leading indicators, lagging indicators, and exceptions." He

---

38 Gino Wickman, *Traction: Get a Grip on Your Business* (BenBella Books, 2011), 122.

leans back in his chair, taking another bite of the soda bread. "Good choice, Tim, by the way. I love this stuff."

"Had to do something to celebrate," Tim says. "My dad's whole side of the family is Irish. I haven't been feeling any Irish luck until recently, though."

"Well, let's keep it going," Barry says. "Let's broach our final topic—scaling. This is the Scalable Business Framework, after all, and I know scaling is one of your main goals for FastTrack."

"Yes, definitely," Tim says enthusiastically, starting a new heading. "I feel like I've been waiting to hear about this for weeks."

"Building systems, scaling your business—everything we've talked about with the Scalable Business Framework—it's all about understanding what success looks like at each step," Barry says sagely. "You don't need to tackle everything at once. Think about the concept of a minimum viable product."

"A what?" Tim asks.

"Basically, it's the minimum requirements to say, 'Yes, this meets my goals for now,'" Barry says. "It's like getting a skateboard, then upgrading to a dirt bike and eventually a truck. The point is to start with what works now and improve as you go. You don't need the finished product right away. You can still get value out of these iterations while you continue to improve."

Tim sits back for a moment, absorbing this. "Right. That's why I had to put my scaling plans on the back burner until I was ready."

"Yes," Barry says. "That's the approach we take when implementing the SBF. You start small, build what you need to meet your current goals, and then iterate over time. That's how you scale a business successfully—through consistent improvements."

"Rome wasn't built in a day," Tim says.

"Well said," Barry confirms, leaning forward. "Also, this is when working with someone who understands both the technology and the business side of things can really help. Working with Charis Strategies and integrating our advice with your own in-house experts, like Wendy, should do the trick for you."

"It's already making a difference," Tim says.

"Assuming you do all that," Barry continues, "the real challenge is getting everything aligned—processes, automation, visibility—and making sure it's all working together. That's why businesses struggle to grow. If you've got a deficit in one of these areas, whether it's a lack of defined processes, hesitation to automate, or a lack of visibility, you're stunting your ability to scale."

The coffee shop is full now, and a few people are loitering, looking hopefully around for tables. Tim and Barry see this and look at each other.

"I think that's about it for today," Barry says. As they begin to vacate their table, he sums up the day's discussion.

"So, to bring it all together, scaling a business requires getting your processes, automation, and visibility aligned. It's about having a clear single source of truth and building systems that enable your team to succeed at every level. And it's not about tackling everything at once—start small, focus on the minimum viable product, and iterate from there."

Tim stands, shouldering his laptop bag. "Thanks, Barry. It's really exciting to see how this all fits together. It makes so much sense."

Barry smiles, hefting his gym bag. "You're already on the right path, Tim. Keep making those decisions, and you'll be amazed at the freedom you create."

"When should we meet again?" Tim asks. "I do have homework to do for next week, after all."

"Why don't we play it by ear?" Barry says. "Email me what you come up with for visibility, and we can meet when you've got a specific process or issue to discuss. In the meantime, our teams can be in contact as you continue to implement the SBF."

"That sounds good," Tim says as the two of them walk out into the sunshine. "I can't wait to see what happens next."

Chapter 12 Summary

Scalable Business Framework: Visibility

Advantages of Visibility
- Adaptability
- Unified information (single source of truth)

Types of Data
- Lagging indicators
- Leading indicators
- Exceptions

Considerations for Gathering Data
- Data capture
- Data structure
- Data access/availability
- Data velocity

Accountability Through KPIs ("Knowing Your Number")
- Each team member must understand their key performance indicators.
- Data access promotes accountability and empowerment.

Scaling Strategies
- Start small with a minimum viable product.
- Focus on consistent, incremental improvements.
- Align processes, automation, and visibility for sustainable scaling.

Learn more about visibility at
ScalableBusinessFramework.com.

Part 4

Impact

Chapter 13

A New Dawn

Fifteen Years Later

It's Christmastime again at La Chance Café. Evergreen garlands frame the windows and drape the counters, and Harper's light pink hair protrudes from a Santa hat. She greets Tim with a friendly wave as he walks in.

"We have a cinnamon cortado, a reindeer red eye, and a mistletoe matcha today," she says.

"What's in the mistletoe matcha?" asks Tim.

"Matcha, obviously," Harper explains, "with oat milk, cloves, coriander, and some rosemary instead of mistletoe. Mistletoe isn't actually edible, you see."

Tim hides a reflexive grimace. "Can I just get my regular, please?" he asks.

"Sure thing," she says. As she rings Tim up, he catches a glimpse of himself in the large mirror behind the counter, noting that his hair has reached real salt-and-pepper status now. He doesn't mind it.

Tim meanders over to his usual seat. Over the past decade and a half, the regulars have learned he likes to sit here, and they're kind enough to steer clear for the most part. It has everything he needs: a power outlet, a cozy corner, and a clear view of the room to see any of the frequent guests who might join him.

Opening his laptop, Tim checks his email to find a virtual Christmas card from Barry. He's on a sailboat with his family, an amazing sunset lighting up the background. It's been several years since he's seen Barry in person, but Tim looks forward to the occasional email about his recent travels and adventures.

Someday this will be me, Tim thinks, smiling as he looks at the photo. With his business thriving now, he knows he'll be able to exit gracefully one day and spend even more time with his family. As it is, they've been scheduling two vacations a year along with almost every weekend off. It turned out he didn't have to sacrifice one part of his life for the other; he could have both.

Unable to help himself, Tim minimizes his email to once again look at his own Christmas card photo for this year. The large group of smiling people in Christmas sweaters sit under a gargantuan Christmas tree. In the center, grinning with their cheeks pressed together, are he and Robin. Their relationship is better than ever, and even the kids, now in college and high school, all managed to smile in this photo.

Tim glances past his computer screen to the second seat at the little table, which sits empty, as though waiting for someone. He lets out a low chuckle, remembering how uncomfortable he was when he first took that seat across from Barry. He was physically uneasy, as he was on the verge of needing to buy larger pants. However, it isn't the physical discomfort that he remembers the most. Tim vividly recalls that uncomfortable, sick feeling of being at rock bottom. He knew he needed help, and felt incredibly vulnerable baring his soul to a successful businessman about a deeply personal issue. Still, he recognized that he needed a lifeline, even if it meant admitting he was in over his head.

Crossing his arms behind his head and leaning back, Tim reflects on the past fifteen years. That moment of vulnerability was a turning point. Thanks to that, Tim learned that vulnerability and self-awareness could turn his failure into success. He learned that providing his team with the right systems and processes empowered them to succeed and even lead.

Within months of Tim and Barry's first meeting, Tim's whole team became intimately familiar with the Scalable Business Framework. And once they recognized its iterative nature and scalability, they really latched on. Everyone, including Tim, was hooked on watching the ideas and processes take shape.

Tim turns back to his laptop, clicking on a familiar tab to open his CRM. Once the ball started rolling, his team did more with his business than he'd ever imagined was possible. FastTrack took on its own identity, an inner life of its own. The culture was unlike anything Tim had ever been a part of, but because of what he learned about leadership, he was able to support his team as they grew the business. He's no longer the ceiling of the business; in fact, it could run efficiently without him.

The CRM's home page shows that revenue continues to grow. Inbound leads from the new channel they launched earlier in the year are beginning to grow as well. A few records are outside the expected standards, so Tim digs a little deeper and sees that the automated notifications have been triggered. His team is on it, and he has full confidence in them. Even better, now that everyone but the technicians are remote, his team is able to enjoy the same flexibility he has found.

"Hey, Tim!" He looks up to see Jackie, a friend of his and Robin's from their running group, striding over with her to-go cup in hand.

"Jackie!" Tim says, rising to shake her free hand. "I really enjoyed our meeting last week. Is your team doing any better?"

"Actually, yes," Jackie says. "Thank you again for explaining your team's process to me last week. It was so eye-opening."

Jackie is the owner of a fast-growing clothing brand called Orange Tiger. When a video of an influencer trying on some Orange Tiger jackets took off on social media,

Jackie's team was suddenly overwhelmed with orders. After she mentioned this during their usual Thursday evening run, Tim offered to meet during the day and show her his sales process. Even though their businesses were different, Tim knew the SBF could help her capitalize on success instead of being crushed by the pressure.

"Glad to help!" Tim says, smiling. "There was actually a lot of other stuff I wanted to show you as well. I'd love to meet again, and it'd be great if you could bring whoever is in charge of sales along too."

"I would absolutely love that," Jackie says, her smile flashing as she whips out her phone. "Can we meet at the same time next week?"

"Absolutely," Tim says, already thinking about everything he wanted to go over with her. "Let's work on getting your team involved in addressing the core process. Remember, those who write the plan don't fight the plan."

"That's a catchy one," says Jackie as she types in the appointment. "Looking forward to it . . . I really can't thank you enough."

As she heads to the door, Tim hears a commotion at the register.

"Shoot, I forgot my wallet," a frazzled man says, patting frantically at his pants pockets. "Of all the days, too. I really needed some caffeine." Behind the counter, Harper is unfazed, waiting for this man to produce his wallet or step out of line for the next guest.

"I got it," Tim says as he moves toward the counter, sliding his credit card over to Harper. She raises her eyebrows, which disappear into the fuzzy rim of her Santa hat.

"That's awfully kind, Tim," she says.

"Are you sure?" asks the stranger, now patting his jacket pockets.

"Absolutely!" says Tim, feeling the Christmas spirit.

"All right," Harper says, taking the card. "Quadruple-shot, extra-hot caramel macchiato coming right up."

Tim glances back at the man. His hair is standing straight up in several spots, and he has what looks like a mustard stain on his white shirt. Even though he's smiling, his eyes have a bloodshot, panicky look Tim remembers all too well.

"Thank you," says the man, holding out a hand. "I'm Ben. Have I seen you here before?"

"I wouldn't be surprised," Tim says, reaching out his hand to shake Ben's. "I'm Tim. Do you work around here?"

Ben nods, "Yeah, this place is on the way to my office. I own an accounting firm. What about you?"

"I'm nearby too," Tim says, sliding his card back into his wallet. "I own FastTrack Home Services; we used to have a place around here. I'm mostly remote now and just really love coming here."

"Oh wow, FastTrack!" Ben says, his bloodshot eyes widening. "I've heard of you guys. You've grown a ton. It's been amazing to watch."

"Thanks," Tim says, grinning. "It's been a blast. My team is just incredible."

Ben slumps against the counter under the pickup sign, which is bedecked with a sprig of holly. "I just don't see how you did it," he says, running a hand through his hair. Tim now understands why that hair is sticking up in so many places. "The more we've grown, the harder it's become," Ben laments. "We seem to have more and more issues every day, and I'm at the center of it all. Maybe I don't have the right team or something . . ." He gnaws his lip absently, staring at the wall.

"You know," says Tim, "I've found that most issues are process issues, not people issues."

"Process issues?" Ben asks vacantly.

"Yeah," Tim says. "Do you have a few minutes? I'd love to hear more about your situation. Maybe I can help."

Ben goggles at Tim. "Wow. Yeah, I'll make time for that," he says. "I need all the help I can get."

Harper slides Ben's drink into his limp hand, rolling her eyes good-naturedly at Tim. Ben's hand closes around the cup reflexively, and he follows Tim back to his table, taking the seat that was sitting empty. Tim has left his laptop open to his email, which shows Barry's e-Christmas card photo.

"It's hard to believe people have adventures like that," Ben says wistfully. "I guess that's the price you pay for owning a business."

Tim suddenly has the most intense sense of déjà vu. He feels as if he knows Ben's story, his struggles, and his fears. He knows how to help this man. It's what Barry did for him, and now he wants to spread the wealth. Maybe *this* is his purpose now.

Tim gives Ben a reassuring look. "This guy," he says, gesturing at the photo, "is one of the most successful businessmen I know. He taught me how to have it all, and I think I can teach you how to have it all too."

Ben's eyes are so wide that both his irises are fully visible. "Oh, man, that sounds great, but I just don't think it's possible for me."

"Let's find out," Tim says, settling back into his chair. "Tell me more about your business. Let's see what we can figure out together."

As Ben begins to chatter away, Tim can't hide his smile. Everything is coming full circle, and all is right with the world.

Conclusion

by Michael A. Johnson

I grew up on a steep hill in my neighborhood. Around age five, when I was learning to ride a bike, I accidentally sped down that hill, tumbled off my bike, and scraped my knees—and my nerves—pretty badly. After that incident, I was scared of getting hurt again and didn't start riding a bike regularly until I was seven.

My friends didn't share this fear and were comfortable riding their bikes long before I was. While I could walk to the cul-de-sac where my friends often played, they were able to go on adventures without me. Behind our neighborhood was a power line right-of-way accessible through a trail in the woods, and my friends would talk about the hills and jumps there. I wanted to join them more than anything, but my fear of near-term pain outweighed my desire for long-term fun.

I remember sitting at the end of the driveway one sunny day, helmet on, thinking, *Can I do this?* I didn't have my training wheels on anymore, and all my friends were on their bikes. I really wanted to join them, but I was hesitant—I wanted to make sure that I wouldn't crash, that I'd do it right. So I just sat there, feeling miserable, nervous, and left out.

What I really needed to do was just get started. I needed to learn along the way and adjust based on those lessons, whether they involved falling or figuring out how to navigate the hill. It wasn't going to be perfect, and I was more likely to make mistakes than to get it right, but heading down that hill was the only path to growth. And eventually I did it.

That's the message I want to leave you with. You've read this book. You know what you need to do. The biggest takeaway now is just to get started.

So often, we hesitate because we're afraid of not having everything figured out, or we let perfection stop us from making progress. The key is not to try to do everything at once. Jump in, learn, and adapt as you go.

If you're ready to bike down that hill, visit our website at ScalableBusinessFramework.com. We'd love to give you the push you need to mount that bike and speed down the path to the Scalable Business Framework.

Afterword

by John Burdett

Thank you for reading this book. It's truly an honor to share many of the lessons I've learned while scaling businesses.

As we wrote this book, I went through one of the most difficult times of my life. In fact, I'm still going through it. But the principles we've shared helped me navigate it with a sense of peace—not just in business, but in life as a whole.

For me, this book reinforced something we talk about often. At the end of the day, people are all that really matter. Relationships, a meaningful family life, good health, and enjoyment of life in all its aspects, without sacrificing one for another, are what truly count.

To give some context, I was diagnosed with ulcerative colitis in December 2017. When I heard those words at the doctor's office, I had no idea what they meant, but I quickly learned that ulcerative colitis is an autoimmune disease that affects the colon. With autoimmune diseases, your body attacks itself. Your own immune system turns against you. Like with many other autoimmune diseases, doctors don't really know what causes it. There's nothing you can do to prevent it.

The good news is that a lot of medications are available to treat it. If you've ever watched TV, you've probably seen commercials for drugs treating autoimmune conditions like ulcerative colitis, psoriasis, and rheumatoid arthritis. It took three or four years to find a medication that worked for me, but once I did, I was fortunate to be in full remission for three years.

Then, in late December 2024, I started feeling sick. I assumed it was just a stomach bug—I hadn't had a flare-up in years. After a few weeks, I realized it was a flare-up. After a month of trying to get it under control, I had a colonoscopy. The doctor was very confident it was ulcerative colitis (they said the entire room verbally gasped when they saw how bad it was), but first he had to send the labs off to confirm it wasn't cancer before approving one of the newer drugs that could hopefully put me back into remission.

At that point, I went back home, but I kept getting worse. A week later, the labs still weren't back and I couldn't wait any longer. I had lost forty pounds from my original, healthy weight and was now emaciated. I couldn't eat. My stomach cramped nonstop. I was constantly nauseated. I even developed a blood clot—a side effect of ulcerative colitis, made worse by the fact that I couldn't move much.

On top of that, I was dealing with all the usual symptoms of the disease (I'll let you Google those).

For the first time in my life, I had to be hospitalized.

The doctors put me on high doses of steroids to get the flare-up under control. They hoped to discharge me from the hospital quickly so I could start the new medication.

I have to pause here because I can't tell this story without sharing how God took care of me. I was actually more comfortable at the hospital than I had been at home. I wasn't comfortable by any means, but at least I had medication to help me get through it.

The biggest miracle in all of this was the peace I felt. Even though this was the hardest thing I had ever been through, by a factor of one hundred, I felt covered by God's peace. I was basically dying—malnourished, dealing with all kinds of complications from the colitis—but my wife, my family, and I had an overwhelming peace through it all.

And this is where people really matter. Strong relationships, close friends, family—those are the things that make the difference. The hardest part was there was nothing anyone could do to help me. It was frustrating for all of them. They wanted to help but couldn't, and that included my wife. She was by my side the entire time and was absolutely amazing, but she was powerless.

Our prayer the whole time was, "God, close the doors that need to be closed, open the doors that need to be opened, and we'll walk through them." And that's exactly what happened.

After two weeks in the hospital, I still wasn't responding to the steroids. By that point, I had lost sixty pounds. This was when it got really tough. The next option was surgery to remove my colon entirely. It wasn't ideal, but I was in such bad shape that there was no other choice. I wasn't responding to treatment, and it was dangerous to stay on such high doses of steroids for too long.

At that point, I was out of options. I couldn't be discharged; I wouldn't survive. And I couldn't wait another two weeks to see if a new drug might work.

Then one of my friends called me.

"Hey, man, I heard what was happening with you, and I think I might be able to help," she said. "My daughter is a colorectal nurse. She's been working under this doctor for the last five years. He's the best in the state, and he goes to our church. Can I pass on your information?"

On top of that, another close friend knew this doctor—let's call him Dr. G—really well. And it turned out he was super close with about ten of my other close friends. Once again, God was taking care of me, helping me make the right decision.

Dr. G had just been recruited to the hospital I was in as head of colorectal surgery. And here's where it gets crazy: The hospital he came from is one of the best in the Southeast, and by far the best in the state.

Why would he leave to come here? And why did he make the move just six weeks before I ended up in this hospital? On top of all that, he was connected to so many people I knew. It's just crazy, right?

That Saturday morning, Dr. G called me. He walked me through everything. The surgery itself is tough, and the recovery process isn't easy, but I would be human again. I would get my life back. And they could actually rewire everything so that I wouldn't have to live with an ostomy bag. I know it sounds rough, but when you've been through what I was going through, this was clearly the right option. My wife and I didn't hesitate.

"Yes, let's do this," I told Dr. G. God had aligned everything in a way that made the decision obvious. I just had to wait a couple of days to wean off some of the medications I was on since I couldn't have the surgery while taking them.

The surgery was super successful. They did it robotically, but they couldn't remove the colon through the robotic incisions because my colon was twice the size it should have been. They had to make a C-section-style cut. Women reading this who've had C-sections can relate—I have that same incision. Not exactly an ideal spot for a cut, but it was necessary to get everything out. It has slowed my recovery a bit, and there have been some challenges, but overall it's been a huge improvement.

The next morning, I was hungry again. I felt normal. Sure, there were side effects from the surgery, but they were *nothing* compared to the pain and suffering I'd been going through.

Within twenty-four hours, I was able to start eating again, and let me tell you—eating has been fun. You don't realize how much you miss the little things. It took me about five days to get out of the hospital. I had some complications, but nothing out of the ordinary.

Now, I'm a little over two and a half weeks out and doing well. The biggest challenge is tapering off the steroids since I was on them for so long, but I'll get back to 100 percent. I have a couple more surgeries ahead, but they're minor compared to this one, and I can do them on my own timeline. Even if I didn't do them, I'd still be in a great place. It's a blessing, and I'm just so grateful. I was looking forward to something as simple as going on a date with my wife, and we've already been able to do that.

Now, this is where I want to tie in the principles we teach in the Scalable Business Framework—principles I've learned throughout my career. And, thank God, I got to benefit from them.

The first is that Fast Slow Motion didn't miss a beat. The business already runs without me, and the team was fully prepared. There was very little I had to do, if anything at all. I never worried about it, and the team handled everything just fine. The conversations we had were more like, "Hey, starting Tuesday, I'll be completely out of pocket for a few days, but you guys have it covered." And they did. The business was already running smoothly without me, so my hiatus was no issue at all. I hadn't been able to work much over the previous ten weeks anyway.

Another great thing is that we've taken on an outside partner at Fast Slow Motion, and it was the same kind of conversation with them. They're the best partners in the world. Their response was simple: "Take care of yourself, and don't worry about the business." One of them even said, "Your business is the one we worry about the least." That kind of confidence and support meant everything, and it's because of the principles we've implemented—the same ones we talk about in this book.

The second principle is health. Taking care of yourself matters. Just like Barry, I was training for a half-marathon with my daughter before all of this happened. I do CrossFit all the time, and while I didn't have sixty pounds to lose, I definitely had a few. I was pretty muscular—now all of that is gone. No muscle, no cardio. I'm super skinny. But I'll be back.

The key is that because I prioritized my health, my body was in a better position to handle what came my way. And that ties into the flexibility principle (part of our core people principle) at Fast Slow Motion. Having the flexibility to work out when I want and stay healthy has been a huge blessing.

Third, and probably most importantly, is having a fully integrated life. My relationships, just like Tim's in the book, weren't always great. You might remember that from the introduction. But because I implemented these principles, they became stronger than I ever could have imagined, and those relationships literally saved my life. Without them, I wouldn't have been connected with Dr. G.

I'll also say this. As I mentioned before, this was by far the hardest thing I've ever been through. But even in it, there was extreme peace, and my wife and I were prepared. Both of our kids are in college, and we were so grateful that we didn't have small kids at home because she could be there with me the entire time. We're financially stable. The business is solid. Everything lined up in a way that allowed us to focus on what mattered.

And because of that, our relationship grew. My relationship with my kids grew. My relationship with God grew. My friendships grew. All of my relationships deepened, and people around me got to see that. My leadership grew because they saw me at a very low point, and I truly believe the lessons I learned in this season are going to make a real impact on others. I can't wait to see how that unfolds.

I want to wrap up with a few key points.

First, everything we talk about in this book is real. I'm living proof, and I've seen it in the lives of our clients.

As Barry mentions throughout the book, don't get caught up in perfection. You can build a business you love while also being a great parent, husband, wife, friend—whatever role you're in—and without missing out on life. You don't have to feel trapped in your business. You can run a highly successful company and still receive the blessings that come with it. So, like Michael Johnson says in the conclusion, I encourage you to get started.

Second, I want to give a huge thank you to Michael. He's been a tremendous blessing to me and to our company. He's the one who created the Scalable Business Framework. I came up with the Three P's, but he took the principles we implemented at Fast Slow Motion and turned them into a real methodology that we now use with clients. He's incredibly talented, and honestly, his name should probably be first in this book.

So, I just want to take a moment to honor Michael. If you ever have questions about the SBF, you're welcome to reach out to me or anyone on our team at ScalableBusinessFramework.com—but to be honest, you'd probably be better off talking to Michael. He's the right guy for that conversation.

Third, if you or someone in your family is dealing with ulcerative colitis, I'd be more than happy to talk with you. I may not have all the answers, but I've lived through the full cycle of it. If you're going through it or know someone who is, please reach out—either through ScalableBusinessFramework.com or on LinkedIn.

This is a tough disease, and it can be incredibly frustrating, especially for someone like me. In the book, I talk about being a fixer, someone who sees problems and immediately looks for solutions. But with this, no matter how much you fight, sometimes you can't win, and that's hard to accept. Some of the medications, the possibility of surgery—it's all overwhelming. And unless you've been through it, it's hard to truly understand.

This experience has given me a lot more empathy. I've never been high on the compassion scale, but I've learned that sometimes fighting harder isn't the answer. So if you need someone to talk to, that offer stands.

Finally, if this book helped you and you're not someone who likes to keep books, please pass it along to someone else. Our goal is to impact as many people as possible. It truly isn't about making money. As we say in the book, money follows impact. If we add value, everything else takes care of itself. So if this book has helped you, consider buying a copy for someone else or recommending it so they can receive the same blessing.

Thank you so much for reading. God bless you, your business, your family, and everything you do. We wish you all the best, and please don't hesitate to reach out if there's anything we can do for you.

Recommended Reading

The books gathered here aren't just references—they're trusted companions that have shaped our thinking and approach throughout this journey. Some you'll recognize from our citations, their insights woven carefully into the chapters you've just read. Others have influenced us more subtly, informing our perspectives in ways too fundamental to attribute to any single passage. What connects them all is their remarkable ability to shift how we see the world and expand what we believe is possible for a scaling company. We're not suggesting you tackle this entire collection at once—that would be overwhelming. Instead, consider this our invitation to continue the exploration we've started together. These are the works we turn to repeatedly—dog-eared and highlighted—when we need clarity or inspiration. Whether you choose one title or eventually read them all, these books form a constellation of thought that extends far beyond what we've created here. The most important step, as with any worthwhile endeavor, is simply to begin.

Belsky, Scott. *Making Ideas Happen: Overcoming the Obstacles Between Vision and Reality*. Penguin Books Ltd., 2011.

Collins, Jim. *Good to Great: Why Some Companies Make the Leap . . . and Others Don't*. Harper Business, 2001.

Collins, Jim. *Turning the Flywheel: A Monograph to Accompany "Good to Great."* Penguin Random House, 2019.

Collins, Jim, and Bill Lazier. *Beyond Entrepreneurship 2.0: Turning Your Business into an Enduring Great Company*. Random House, 2020.

Collins, Jim, and Jerry I. Porras. *Built to Last: Successful Habits of Visionary Companies*. Random House Business Books, 2005.

Covey, Stephen R. *The Seven Habits of Highly Effective People*. G.K. Hall, 1997.

Drucker, Peter F. *Management: Tasks, Responsibilities, Practices*. Harper & Row, 1973.

Gerber, Michael E. *The E-Myth Revisited: Why Most Small Businesses Don't Work and What to Do About It*. Harper Business, 1995.

Lencioni, Patrick M. *The Advantage: Why Organizational Health Trumps Everything Else In Business*. Josey-Bass, 2012

Maxwell, John C. *The 21 Indispensable Qualities of a Leader: Becoming the Person Others Will Want to Follow.* HarperCollins Leadership, 2007.

Maxwell, John C. *The 21 Irrefutable Laws of Leadership: Follow Them and People Will Follow You.* Thomas Nelson, 1998.

Sinek, Simon. *The Infinite Game.* Portfolio, 2019.

Scott, Kim. *Radical Candor: Be a Kick-Ass Boss Without Losing Your Humanity.* St. Martin's Press, 2017.

Terrance, Zane *17 Reasons Your Company Is Not Investment Grade & What To Do About It.* Own Purpose Publishing, 2020

Tiede, Bob. *Now That's a Great Question: How to Lead with Questions to Build Relationships and Get Results.* Self-published, 2020.

Wickman, Gino. *Traction: Get a Grip on Your Business.* Expanded edition. BenBella Books, 2012.

Wiseman, Liz, and Greg McKeown. *Multipliers: How the Best Leaders Make Everyone Smarter.* HarperCollins, 2010.

About the Authors

**John Burdett** is the CEO and Founder of Fast Slow Motion, a consulting firm that specializes in helping businesses grow and scale using Salesforce and HubSpot. Since Burdett founded the company in 2014, it has grown to a fully remote team of more than 120 people and has completed more than 2,400 projects for over 1,200 clients and counting across the US. For six consecutive years, Fast Slow Motion has appeared on the Inc. 5000 list of the fastest-growing private companies in America.

The success of Fast Slow Motion is the direct result of hard-won lessons Burdett learned throughout his entrepreneurial journey. After helping start and grow multiple companies, he realized he had a unique gift for helping others do the same. "The most pivotal moment in my career was when I realized my calling—to help other people build their businesses using scalable systems and processes. This was the reason I started Fast Slow Motion," Burdett says. "I had already made every mistake possible in business, and learned along the way. I realized I could help others avoid making the same mistakes and grow their businesses the *right* way."

When it comes to building businesses, Burdett measures success in more than just financial metrics. One of his deeply held values is that "people matter most," and he is passionate about fostering meaningful lives for business leaders, their families, and employees. Within his own company, creating a vibrant culture in which employees can live "fully integrated" lives has been a labor of love, with lessons that are more relevant than ever for both in-person and remote teams.

In addition to demonstrating how a well-built business can improve both the financial and personal lives of everyone it touches, Burdett also models how business leaders can further compound the positive impacts they create in a community. He is the co-founder of an innovative organization called Red Mountain Grace, which provides housing for the families of patients receiving medical care in Fast Slow Motion's hometown of Birmingham, Alabama.

Burdett's blend of business acumen and compassion makes him a sought-after voice in discussions on building sustainable operations and nurturing positive workplace cultures. He offers real-world wisdom and practical guidance on how to build a thriving business with immense purpose while still enjoying life.

Michael Johnson is the expert every entrepreneur wants on their team when it's time to grow their business. Since 2010, Michael has helped hundreds of businesses across dozens of industries build scalable systems using CRM technology. The teams he has led throughout his career have helped organizations, ranging in size from ten employees to 10,000, standardize and streamline their processes and position themselves for growth.

Michael has worked in the trenches of marketing, sales, e-commerce, and technology, witnessing firsthand the role that good processes coupled with strong technology play in the success of a business. In his current role as Director of Growth at Fast Slow Motion, Michael is one of FSM's chief evangelists, on a mission to help businesses grow and scale using CRM platforms.

With an engaging, personable style, Michael draws on his in-depth expertise to help audiences:

- Understand the practical considerations and benefits of building scalable systems.

- Unlock the right systems to create success and freedom.
- Learn best practices for implementing CRMs and standardizing business processes.
- Take the next right step in growing their businesses.

Michael regularly appears on a variety of podcasts and at live events throughout, sharing his wisdom on building scalable systems and helping businesses grow the right way.

Made in the USA
Columbia, SC
22 November 2025